Discipleship That Works

The LampPost Strategy for Disciplemaking

GRANT EDWARDS

Discipleship That Works: The LampPost Strategy for Disciplemaking
Copyright © 2024, 2025 Grant C. Edwards

All rights reserved. No part of this book may be reproduced in any manner whatsoever without prior written permission from the publisher except where noted in the text and in the case of brief quotations embedded in critical articles, reviews, books, and electronic publications. Email for permission to GrantEdwardsAuthor@gmail.com. Or write Permissions at Specificity Publications, 1357 Greystone Drive, Springfield, OH 45503.

Visit our website: GrantEdwardsAuthor.com

Credits
Creative: Mikal Keefer
Editor: Sharon Wildman
Art Director: Barbara Edwards

Scripture quotations marked (ESV) are taken from the ESV® Bible (The Holy Bible, English Standard Version®). Copyright © 2001 by Crossway, a publishing ministry of Good News Publishers. Used by permission All rights reserved.

Scripture quotations marked (NLT) are taken from the Holy Bible, New Living Translation. Copyright © 1996, 2004, 2015 by Tyndale House Foundation. Used by permission of Tyndale House Ministries, Carol Stream, Illinois 60188. All rights reserved.

Scripture quotations marked (NASB1995) are taken from the New American Standard Bible, Copyright © 1960, 1962, 1963, 1968, 1971, 1972, 1973, 1975, 1977, 1995 by The Lockman Foundation. Used by permission. www.Lockman.org

Scripture quotations marked (NIV) are taken from the Holy Bible, New International Version® NIV®. Copyright © 1973, 1978, 1984, 2011 by Biblica, Inc.® Used by permission of Zondervan. All rights reserved worldwide. www.zondervan.com. The "NIV" and "New International Version" are trademarks registered in the United States Patent and Trademark Office by Biblica, Inc.®

Scripture quotations marked (NET) are from the NET Bible®. https://netbible.com. Copyright © 1996, 2019. Used with permission from Biblical Studies Press, LLC All rights reserved.

ISBN: 979-8-9887086-1-2 (Paperback)

Table of Contents

Introduction 7

Chapter 1: The Problem 9
   Interlude # 1: Lamp Posts in Colonial America 18

Chapter 2: Know the Right Definition and Content 21
   Interlude #2: Origins of Disciplemaking 28

Chapter 3: Read the Blueprint! 31
   Interlude #3: Two Houses 44

Chapter 4: Things Ya Do and Things Ya Don't Do! 45
   Interlude #4: Seinfeld and Conversational Script 57

Chapter 5: I Can Do This! 59
   Interlude #5: The Lost Art of Disciplemaking 72

Chapter 6: The LampPost Strategy 75
   Interlude #6: The Test 86

Chapter 7: Content ~ Same for the Foundation, Different for the Formation 89
   Interlude #7: Orphans 99

Chapter 8: A Culture of Sustainable Disciplemaking 101
   Interlude #8: You Can Do This! 115

Chapter 9: Making the Connection 117
   Interlude #9: Law of Supply and Demand 128

Chapter 10: Revolution 131
   Interlude #10: Albert Einstein and Disciplemaking 144

Chapter 11: 3rd Generation Disciplers 147
    Interlude #11: Wave Theory of Change 166

Chapter 12: 90 Days 169
    Interlude #12: 90-Day Cycles 181

Chapter 13: Would You Know What to Do? 183
    Interlude #13: The First Meeting 199

Chapter 14: "Yes" or "No"? 203

Endnotes 217
About the Author 221

Acknowledgments

I began discipling within a month of becoming a follower of Jesus. This book reflects what I have learned in fifty years of disciplemaking. With a long path of learned best practices in my calling to disciple, it would be difficult to name all the contributors who have influenced and encouraged my thinking.

I thank my wife, Barbara, who has great ideas and also contributes her graphic designs in this book and with my blog *Interruptions* at GrantEdwardsAuthor.com.

Writing this book, I penned 300,000 words, and only 50,000 made the final edit. I thank Mikal Keefer, a friend, writer, and great editor, for helping me reduce and hone my thoughts. I'm certain that you will enjoy reading 50,000 words rather than 300,000!

This book took three years to write. I had a lifetime of thoughts to consider and new research about changing the culture of a church to reflect one-to-one disciplemaking.

All of this material needed focus. I needed an ally.

Thank you, Sharon Wildman, for coming alongside. I've known Sharon for fifty years, and she has used my material for decades in discipling dozens. This experience, along with her editing skills, added depth to this book.

After I left my role as a senior pastor for forty-nine years to launch First Steps Discipleship a team of talented co-workers have given many hours to consultation, encouragement, and insight into writing this book. Thank you Rick and Heather Ives, Bud Downing, Richard Wildman, and Dr. Ron Braley.

Two years ago, a local businessman wanted to help me find more time to write. He asked if he could provide management assistance for one of my personal business ventures. Thank you, Gary Durst, for your support.

Introduction

Jesus spoke to them, saying, "I am the light of the world. Whoever follows me will not walk in darkness, but will have the light of life" (John 8:12, ESV).

There is no greater need in the church today than discipleship that works.

Today, more than ever, plenty of books, conferences, blogs, and podcasts discuss discipleship. But are we doing better at disciplemaking?

This abundance of disciplemaking material doesn't equal more success. I constantly hear church leaders asking, "What should I do? Which plan works? Which writer has the best approach?"

With bold humility, I answer this way: I do. That's why I've written this book entitled *Discipleship That Works*!

Before you accuse me of being a lunatic or greatly misguided, know this: I've discipled hundreds of followers of Jesus using the principles and material described in this book. Those people I discipled have discipled thousands more.

I know what I share in this book works. I also believe you can do this too!

There's a damaging statement that hinders discipleship I hear uttered by well-meaning teachers, pastors, church leaders, and writers. The statement is: "There are many approaches to discipleship; just go ahead and choose one."

I have six grandchildren.

Raising these children, my daughters didn't take the "just choose any path" approach. They knew, as you know, there are established developmental issues and goals that are shared by all newborns. There are physical and emotional foundations that must be laid if children are to be healthy.

If we carefully observe newborn followers of Jesus, we quickly note there's a foundation they all need, too. When we nurture new believers with the same foundational disciplines and help them confront the same temptations we all encounter, we're doing discipleship that works. They have the foundation needed to be spiritually healthy.

I want to encourage you—especially if you've tried to disciple others and haven't had success.

Many have tried and failed in discipleship. Individual believers try to disciple and are frustrated with the results. Churches promote differing plans, sometimes trying one program and then another, with little effect.

Don't give up.

There's a strategy for discipleship that works. I call it *The LampPost Strategy*. This book explains that strategy and provides practical advice for implementing disciplemaking personally and in your church.

Read this book, implement the strategy, and let me know if you agree with the title: *Discipleship That Works!*

You can do this!

Chapter 1:

The Problem

Go therefore and make disciples of all nations! (Matthew 28:19, ESV)

My Story . . .

When I was in the fifth grade, I decided not to follow Jesus.

I had accepted Jesus at Bible camp during the summer, but on the first day of school in the fifth grade, looking around my classroom and realizing there were no other believers, I thought, "If I stay a Christian, I won't have any friends."

Having friends was more important than Jesus.

I stayed faithful to my decision. During my middle and high school years, I followed the "any" philosophy: anything, anytime, anywhere, and I didn't care what anyone thought.

My decision ended with me as a paranoid, suicidal drug user standing on Daytona Beach, Florida, on New Year's Eve 1971/1972. While I was deciding if life was worth it, God sent a long-haired and unkempt group of Jesus Freaks to my rescue.

They told me Jesus didn't mind if I had rejected Him previously, and in fact, it didn't matter what I had done during the previous few years because grace covered it all. Though I was faithless to Jesus, He was faithful to me!

I was baptized in the Atlantic Ocean at midnight that New Year's Eve.

A few days later, I hitchhiked from Florida to my hometown of Springfield, Ohio.

After my profession of "non-belief" in the fifth grade, I became a pagan of pagans and was also a leader of pagans. Many of those in my high school were now doing drugs because of my influence.

I traveled back to Ohio to tell them about true freedom—Jesus. My intention was to share the gospel and then return to the ministry run by the Jesus Freaks in Daytona Beach.

I called my friends, and sixteen of them showed up to meet me. Honestly, I believe they thought I had some type of new drug from Florida. So they were *very* excited to see me. I told them about Jesus. Everyone in the room sat and listened as I described my conversion. Everyone knew me in high school, and now I was professing Jesus. After I finished my testimony, I asked if anyone would like to follow Jesus, and all sixteen raised their hands.

I continued to share my testimony with others, and in three months, one hundred people prayed to become followers of Jesus. Within three years, that number increased to five hundred.

My best friend in high school, one of the original sixteen, told me, "You can't leave Springfield; there are too many people dependent on you."

I never made it back to Florida.

And something else began to happen frequently.

Many of those who had decided to follow Jesus walked away from faithfulness. Whereas there is nothing more exciting in being used by God, there's nothing more frustrating than watching those new believers soon shrug their shoulders and drift away.

I was only months old in the Lord. I was doing drugs just weeks previously. I didn't have a Bible college or seminary degree.

But what could I do?

My adventure with discipleship began!

80 Percent

Eighty percent of those who begin to follow Jesus walk away from faithfulness soon after making their decision—often within three months.

I noticed this within a few months of becoming a follower of Jesus.

I admit my 80 percent statistic is more anecdotal than the result of qualitative or quantitative research. The statistic can be debated, but I believe that if evangelists, book publishers, pastors of megachurches or country churches, blog writers, podcast producers, and anyone organizing a discipleship conference would pause and think . . . I believe they'd agree with this number.

Far too many are walking away from faithfulness.

When I first started leading a ministry, I thought the problem was unique to me, that being young and inexperienced, I should expect this result.

> *Far too many are walking away from faithfulness.*

So I admitted the problem and began reading my Bible, hoping to find a solution.

In the early 1970s, I could find only a few books written about discipleship. Those I found were often too theoretical to be of practical help. And while a church I attended had a new member's class, learning about tithing and denominational doctrines wasn't helpful for a herd of ex-hippies.

I read the Bible over and over. Mostly the New Testament, since I thought it would be more relevant to new believers than all those numbers in the book of Numbers or laws in Deuteronomy.

For six months, I kept this schedule:

- Get up in the morning.
- Spend three hours reading the Bible, focusing on disciplemaking, and even writing discipleship lessons.
- Street witness in the afternoon.

- Use the lessons learned and written in the morning to disciple new followers at night.
- Get up the next day and repeat.

The Light of Discipleship

It didn't take long to discover this passage:

> *Jesus came and said to them, "All authority in heaven and on earth has been given to me. Go therefore and make disciples of all nations, baptizing them in the name of the Father and of the Son and of the Holy Spirit, teaching them to observe all that I have commanded you. And behold, I am with you always, to the end of the age."* (Matthew 28:18–20, ESV)

I remember the jolt of inspiration when I first read this commission. The passage was a command to go and make disciples, but I had questions as I read and re-read the Great Commission along with the rest of the New Testament.

- What does it mean to make disciples?
- How do I do it?
- What do I teach those I'm discipling?

I've been asking these same questions for over fifty years. What I've found is shared in this book. I call the strategy—and it's constantly evolving still—*The LampPost Strategy*.

LampPost Rule #1: Admit the problem.

That 80 percent walk-away number is found in every church, every crusade, every denomination, and every revival.

It's a number considered "unmentionable" in the church. Rather than grapple with that reality, we deny the facts, change Jesus' command from "make disciples" to a more tolerable "share the gospel," and construct bigger and better buildings while forgetting to develop the depth of our relationship with Jesus.

It's like we've checked out and gone to open a bike shop.

Opening a Bike Shop Analogy

For years, I've had a secret fantasy to open a bike shop.

During my decades as a pastor, I thought about it whenever someone got angry with me or said my sermons were too long. The bike shop was a "go-to" dream whenever someone left the church because the music was too loud.

I pictured myself selling Trek® bikes in a small Hallmark®-style village.

But then I realized why I wouldn't be starting a bike shop: I'm not a mechanic. I could sell bikes but not fix them. My customers would storm out in frustration after hearing my sales pitch, purchasing a bike, and then being unable to get the chain adjusted properly.

That's a bit like the church today—good at selling the gospel but less able to fix what's broken.

As a young pastor, when I noticed that 80 percent of my customers often walked away from faithfulness, I asked around and found it wasn't just because I was a novice church leader. *New believers were walking away from Jesus everywhere, and there was very little success in fixing the problem.*

Here's the truth: the modern church is great at reaching the lost but not so good at keeping the saved.

I've recently been in contact with Dr. Ron Braley, who wrote his doctoral thesis on discipleship at Regent University in Virginia Beach. His research included the following sobering information:

Evangelist Ray Comfort writes about his crusades in the 1970s . . .

In the late 1970s, I began an itinerant ministry and found that I had access to church growth records. To my horror, I discovered that evangelistic success wasn't what it was cracked up to be. Modern evangelism, from large campaigns to small gospel meetings, boasted only a 20 percent holding rate. We were creating eighty backsliders for every one hundred "decisions for Jesus."[1]

Eternity magazine reported in 1977 the results of an evangelistic crusade that involved 178 churches . . .

Out of 4,106 decisions, only 3% joined a local church. A year later, only 6% had significantly changed their lives.[2]

In his 2007 book, *UnChristian*, David Kinnaman writes . . .

Our research shows that most of those who made a decision for Christ were no longer connected to a Christian church within a short period, usually eight to twelve weeks, after their initial decision. In a get-saved culture, too many of the conversions become either "aborted" believers or casual Christians. How do we convey to people both the gravity and buoyancy of the decision to follow Christ?[3]

In a report the Barna Organization did for Navigators in 2015 (*The State of Discipleship*), it was discovered that when asked how discipleship was going, church leaders candidly admitted that:

Only 1 percent of today's churches are doing well at discipling new and young believers.[4]

I think again about opening that bike shop every time I read statistics like these about the effectiveness of the church's current discipleship practices.

And it's not just American churches that are struggling. It's all around the world.

When I told a key leader in a large organization that plants churches in India about this "80 percent leave while only 20 percent stay" statistic, he nodded in agreement. "We aren't doing well with discipleship," he admitted. "I agree with the 80 percent statistic."

While teaching discipleship in Novosibirsk, Russia, I told a pastor about my 80 percent statistic, and he asked his church administrator to tally all the conversions in their church during the last two years. The pastor was stunned when his administrator told him, "Only about 20 percent remain."

Unlike the early 1970s when few resources or books were available on the topic of discipleship, today, thousands of books, videos, and internet resources can be found. The cost ranges from free to thousands of dollars, and if you can't find a resource that fits your congregation, it's easy to hire consultants to customize a discipleship program for your specific church.

Are the new programs working? Some are more than others, but a report by Discipleship Lab querying 3,832 church leaders in February 2021 provides the following statistics:

- 92 percent of church leaders strongly believe that the Great Commission is still an important call on their church.
- 53 percent said they had no substantive discipleship wins to point to in the last year.
- 42 percent of those same leaders are not confident in their church's ability to make disciples in the future. [5]

Wow . . . maybe more church leaders are considering opening bike shops!

That believers walk away soon after deciding to follow Jesus isn't a secret. But the response baffles me as many churches admit to needing better discipleship but continue to do what they've always done.

They essentially do . . . nothing.

I recently had an email exchange with Braley and asked him about the 80 percent rate. Ron is one of the few scholars who's studied this topic. I wanted to get his take on this issue.

My question to Braley was:

"One of the points I'm making in my new book is that 80 percent of those who accept Jesus walk away from faithfulness within three months after conversion. Would you agree?"

Braley's more-expert-than-I-am response was:

"Statistics included in my dissertation suggest that nearly all people who 'make a decision' fall away soon after, presumably because no one has walked with them in a discipleship rhythm. So, I think your 80 percent could be optimistic."

So, I think your 80 percent could be optimistic!

Should we sell Trek® or Cannondale® bikes at our bike shop in the small Hallmark®-style village?

I don't believe we have to settle for 20 percent of new converts sticking with Jesus. If Jesus gave us a Great Commission and promised His authority and presence when we disciple others, we ought to *keep* 80 percent.

If we can learn to fix bicycles correctly and keep cycling customers happy, why can't we disciple those who accept Jesus?

> **We can't disciple effectively unless we understand what discipleship means.**

The key is defining "discipleship" correctly. We can't disciple effectively unless we understand what discipleship means.

We'll define "discipleship" in the next chapter, but after the brief review below, we'll pause first as we take an interlude to discover the origin of the first lamp post in the USA.

Chapter 1: The Problem

Review:

- LampPost Rule #1: Admit the problem.

Interlude #1:

Lamp Posts in Colonial America

You are the light of the world! (Matthew 5:14, ESV)

Benjamin Franklin loved the idea of lamp posts. While visiting London, England, Franklin enjoyed seeing where he was walking and what he was stepping into at night. Lighted streets seemed like a no-brainer, but in the city of Philadelphia, where he lived, the idea wasn't generating enthusiasm.

A key reason was that the lamp posts in London didn't work well. They were a single globe that needed to be totally replaced if they were broken. And the air didn't circulate well in them. When lit at dusk, the globe became clouded with soot in a few hours.

The lamps broke easily, didn't work well, and needed to be cleaned daily.

So Benjamin Franklin redesigned the lamp.

He built one with four panes of glass—if one broke, it could easily be replaced. His lamp had holes in the bottom and the top for ventilation, and he designed his lamp with a smaller bottom and larger top that allowed smoke to rise and leave quickly.

His lamp post would shine all night and rarely needed to be cleaned.

Only one difficulty was left. He had a better lamp post, but few seemed to be interested.

Legend has it that he solved this problem by placing his lamp outside his home. Neighbors noticed, others in the city noticed, and soon, the city of Philadelphia had lamp posts. Other cities in the United

States took notice, and street lighting became common everywhere in Colonial America.

Benjamin Franklin redesigned the lamp post, and it became the light of the nation at night.

The Early Church

> *And awe came upon every soul, and many wonders and signs were being done through the apostles. And all who believed were together and had all things in common. And they were selling their possessions and belongings and distributing the proceeds to all, as any had need. And day by day, attending the temple together and breaking bread in their homes, they received their food with glad and generous hearts, praising God and having favor with all the people. And the Lord added to their number day by day those who were being saved.* (Acts 2:43–47, ESV)

Chapter 2:

Know the Right Definition and Content

By this my Father is glorified, that you bear much fruit and so prove to be my disciples. (John 15:8, ESV)

A painter paints. A singer sings. And a disciple disciples.

We aren't surprised to see masterpieces of paintings by Rembrandt displayed in museums around the world. When music devotees discuss the most influential singers in the last one hundred years, Louis Armstrong often tops the lists.

A painter paints. A singer sings.

As a disciple of Jesus, the Apostle Paul followed Jesus and had disciples too. As a disciple of Jesus, I follow the examples of Jesus and Paul to disciple new and renewed followers of Jesus.

A disciple disciples!

But do you disciple? Do you know how to disciple? Do most followers of Jesus disciple?

A Dean of Students at a Seminary

I was sitting on a plane flying to Russia. I was traveling to train pastors and church leaders about one-to-one discipleship in St. Petersburg.

Behind me on the plane sat the dean of students of a large American seminary. He was on our team more out of an interest in visiting Russia than discipleship.

During our conversation on the plane, I asked him, "Let's say you are to disciple a new believer. Knowing there's an 80 percent chance this new follower will walk away from faithfulness in the first three months after accepting Jesus, do you know exactly what to do to maximize the chances that this new believer will last the three months?"

The dean of students looked at me and said, "No, I don't."

At least he was honest.

What's a Disciple to Do?

Let's consider two passages of Scripture:

> *Go therefore and make disciples of all nations, baptizing them in the name of the Father and of the Son and of the Holy Spirit.* (Matthew 28:19, ESV)

> *By this my Father is glorified, that you bear much fruit and so prove to be my disciples.* (John 15:8, ESV)

In English, "make disciples" in Matthew 28:19 is obviously two words, but it is one word in the Greek of the New Testament and translated into English as "make disciples." I believe the best definition of this one word is "disciplemaker!"

A disciple disciples!

In John 15:8, Jesus says that we are to "prove" we are His disciples by bearing much fruit.

In Galatians 5, the Apostle Paul discusses the "fruit of the Spirit." This does indicate spiritual maturity, but is this "maturity" the only definition of the fruit mentioned by Jesus in John 15? Or does "bearing much fruit" in John 15 also define the Great Commission in Matthew 28?

When Jesus says, "bear much fruit and so prove to be my disciples," He could also be saying, "Go, therefore, and be a disciplemaker of all nations."

If a student studies, a swimmer swims, and a college professor professes, it's not a stretch to say that a disciple disciples.

So let's answer the same question I asked the dean of students:

"If we're given a new follower of Jesus to disciple, do we know what to do in the first three months of this new follower's walk with Jesus?"

Most of us don't because we define discipleship incorrectly.

An Oft Used and Wrong Definition

I formed my definition of discipleship based on the Scripture I read, what I learned by observing new believers, and my own experiences of discipling.

It's the definition I've lived with and by for decades—and it's probably not an exact match with what you've seen in print or heard in other places.

Studies today indicate that most church leaders define discipleship as *becoming more Christ-like.* One study says that the top-ranked description of discipleship among Christians is—a *lifelong process and journey rooted in a relationship with Jesus.*[6]

With this definition, we instantly have the problem of deciding *what exactly is more Christ-like?* Is it prayer and Bible study for an hour each morning? Memorizing Scripture? Giving tithes and offerings?

We get the picture: it's nearly impossible to quantify what it means to "become more Christ-like."

And with "becoming more Christ-like" as the definition of discipleship, the content and process of discipleship reflects whatever an individual or denomination considers to be more Christ-like.

Should we teach a new believer about baptism? Is part of discipleship learning about and agreeing with the vision and mission of our church? How about doctrine?

And how do we assess successful discipleship? We can give a test on doctrine, but that's more for seminarians than new believers. We can count the number of verses someone has memorized, but what does that really tell us? The devil can quote Scripture too.

It's a hard-to-define mess.

Considering all of this, I define discipleship as . . . *disciplers discipling disciplers!*

> **I define discipleship as . . . disciplers discipling disciplers!**

Yes, for the Oxford English Dictionary purists, I have just defied the rule of making good definitions by using the word defined in the definition itself. Not only once but three times.

Disciplers discipling disciplers! Like fingernails scratching a chalkboard for librarians. I apologize.

I broke the rule because a disciple should be a disciplemaker. That's the inherent definition of a disciple. As followers of Jesus, if we want to obey Him as our Lord and Savior, we must obey His last command to go and make disciples.

It's easy to know if someone is discipling—just ask them. But, when you do, it leads to the most difficult questions of all.

- How do we disciple?
- What is the best method of discipleship?
- What is the best content for discipleship?

This is LampPost Rule #2: Know the right definition and content.

There are many books on the topic of Christian discipleship listed on Kindle. Many options . . . but which one is best?

After defining discipleship, I found that discipleship should focus on the first three months and that second, a plan for discipleship does exist.

First: Focus on the first three months.

Obviously, with an 80 percent walk-away rate in the first three months of a new believer's faith in Jesus, the first three months should be the emphasis for successful discipleship. Worldwide, Christianity has a fishing net with an 80 percent hole in it, so discipleship must be mended.

The question is, how?

And the answer is *disciplers discipling disciplers.*

When discipleship becomes focused on the first three months, it becomes evident that the best method for discipleship is one-to-one. The dynamics of initial spiritual formation with new believers works best in the context of personal relationships.

I'll discuss this more in the next few chapters.

Second: I found a plan that is most effective.

For me, finding a plan that works was difficult. And identifying the absolute best practices for initial, in-the-first-three-months disciplemaking was seemingly impossible.

Why?

Because I was told over and over that such a plan didn't exist.

As a young believer and leader of ex-hippies who were new followers of Jesus, I needed to know exactly how to disciple these new followers in the first three months. But I was constantly told by authors of books, older pastors, conference speakers, and seminary professors that *"Such a plan doesn't exist! There are many paths of disciplemaking, so just pick what is best for you."*

Early in my studies of the Bible, I read a concept taught by Jesus that I found necessary for the first three months of discipleship.

> *Everyone then who hears these words of mine and does them will be like a wise man who built his house on the rock. And the rain fell, and the floods came, and the winds blew and beat on that house, but it did not fall, because it had been founded on the rock.* (Matthew 7:24–25, ESV)

After reading and memorizing this passage, every time I heard or read the statement, *"There are many ways to disciple, just pick one,"* I knew it was wrong. Jesus said we should build upon the right foundation.

And all foundations have a specific plan.

Every building built in the history of the world has a foundation. And every foundation follows the same rules of construction. When Jesus implied that all believers should have a foundation, then *a specific plan for disciplemaking should exist, especially in the initial three months!*

Jesus did not say, "Just pick the right foundation for you." He said to build upon the rock! Jesus had a plan for discipleship.

And yes, we will discuss this plan in detail in the following chapters. Let's remember:

- The best definition of discipleship is *disciplers discipling disciplers*!
- The best focus of discipleship should be the first three months.
- The best plan for foundational discipleships exists!

These three concepts are why I titled this book *Discipleship That Works!*

Today, we have more discipleship material than ever. Yet the 80 percent walk-away rate hasn't been lowered.

Defining discipleship as non-descript "growing in Christ" and asserting that a plan for initial discipleship doesn't exist will not increase effective discipleship. We build on sand if we lack clear blueprints during the construction of new believers.

> **Do you know exactly what to do with a new believer in the first three months?**

Understanding the correct definition of discipleship and knowing best practices for one-to-one initial disciplemaking will give us confidence when asked, "Do you know exactly what to do with a new believer in the first three months?"

We can respond with, "Yes, absolutely!"

A discipler disciples disciplers.

Chapter 2: Know the Right Definition and Content

Review:
- LampPost Rule #1: Admit the problem.
- LampPost Rule #2: Know the right definition and content.

Before Chapter 3, read *Interlude #2* for a brief history of discipleship.

Interlude #2:

Origins of Disciplemaking

He said to them, "Follow me, and I will make you fishers of men." (Matthew 4:19, ESV)

The Greek word for disciple is *mathetes*. The word is found about 250 times in the New Testament.

The method of discipling found in the Gospels isn't found in the Old Testament.

With the word for disciple mentioned only in the Gospels and the book of Acts but not in the letters of the New Testament, and with no Jesus-style discipling in the Old Testament, I've asked myself, "Am I a loon for emphasizing disciplemaking as a primary feature of the Bible?"

Let's consider the origins of first-century disciplemaking.

Discipling Isn't Found in the Old Testament

Yes, Joshua stayed at the Tent of Meeting to bask in God's glory after Moses met with God. Joshua did succeed Moses, but there is no evidence of a "follow me" relationship between Moses and him. Elisha did follow Elijah around Israel, and Elijah's mantle fell to Elisha, but there's nothing about a close discipling relationship between them.

There were bands of Old Testament prophets, but it was based upon God's revelation to each prophet, with no prophetic school of major prophets discipling upcoming minor prophets.

Where did the idea of disciplemaking originate?

Probably from Socrates and his disciple Plato, as both had a desire to disciple students by relational learning and not mere teaching of pupils. The Pharisees and Sadducees adopted the Greek practice of this teacher/disciple training.

Jewish and Greek disciples were allowed to follow their teachers because of their qualifications of ability, cultural status, and wealth. Saul (changed to Paul) came from an influential family in Tarsus who were also Roman citizens.

With both the Greeks and Jews, there would be no acceptance letters to their schools of discipleship for lowly fishermen and, especially, tax collectors. The rest of the disciples of Jesus wouldn't qualify either.

Jesus practiced discipling (common during His time), but He considerably changed the practice.

The Apostle Paul writes in Galatians that Jesus came in the fullness of time (Galatians 4:4). This fullness of time had (for the first time in history) created a worldwide empire with a system of travel, similar culture, the *Pax Romana* of peace, and a common language in which the gospel could spread. But another "fullness of time" change was that disciplemaking was already accepted and practiced.

Jesus just had to adapt it.

How?

First, disciples of Greek philosophers, along with the Pharisees and Sadducees, attached *themselves* to their teacher. But Jesus called the twelve to *"Follow me!"*

Second, the Pharisees and Sadducees promoted a certain system of thought. Sadducees discipled Sadducees, and Pharisees discipled Pharisees. However, Jesus offered Himself as both the teacher and the topic while saying, *"Follow me!"* Jesus was the Way, the Truth, and the Life!

Third, the disciplemaking of the Pharisees and Sadducees taught allegiance to a way of works and law, but Jesus taught a "follow me" that led to a relationship with God.

The "follow me" discipleship with Jesus meant that His disciples didn't learn a system of beliefs or emulate a set of religious rules, but they walked with the Lord of Life Himself.

This new manner of discipling was the cause of the actual word "disciple" disappearing from the last half of the New Testament. The word changed from "disciple" to saints, believers, co-workers, and Christians—words that wouldn't be confused with the Greek and Jewish practices of discipling.

The diminishing usage of the word "disciple" in the New Testament did not negate the Great Commission of Jesus, as the entire New Testament promoted the principles of one-to-one disciplemaking.

Discipleship is still the foundational practice through which a new believer learns to live the exchanged life with Jesus.

Jesus still says to all of us, *"Follow me!"*

Chapter 3:

Read the Blueprint!

It did not fall, because it had been founded on the rock. (Matthew 7:25, ESV)

Decades ago, I was thinking about foundations and discipleship. I had just read Matthew 7:24–27 about the wise man building his house upon the rock and looked up the word "build" in the Greek. One commentator said, "The word properly meant to build up from the foundation."[7]

I thought, "If I'm discipling a person, and I build them properly, then I should start with the foundation and build the house on top of this foundation."

This made perfect sense.

About that time, a friend told me that his wife's parents were building a lake house. They lived in another part of the state and couldn't watch the laying of the foundation.

When they arrived a few weeks into the construction, they saw their house completely framed with roofers nailing shingles on the roof. They also quickly noted that the house was turned around backward.

It is easier to do with a lake house, as the front of the house was designed to face the lake and not the street. But it would not have happened had the builder correctly read the blueprints for the foundation!

The foundation blueprints correctly displayed the house facing the lake.

Oops!

The spiritual maturity of all believers must have the right foundation.

As I thought about building the right foundation and the story of the house built backward, I kept thinking that the foundation comes first, and then building the actual house comes later.

The foundation must be right, or the house built on top of it will be an "Oops!"

The foundation for all believers looks the same, but the formation of the houses built on similar foundations is different for all believers. This was the errant builder's problem, as he had never built a house with the back facing the road and the front facing another direction.

He didn't connect the right foundation with the house he was building.

In disciplemaking, there is both foundational *and* formational discipleship. And the right foundation must be in place for future spiritual formation.

When new houses are built, their foundations are the same—they should just be built in the right direction! But the formations of houses differ. A Victorian house and a ranch house have similar foundations but look completely different above ground.

> **The foundation is the same . . . but the formation is different for every believer.**

During the process of new believers growing in Christ, the foundation is the same for all followers of Jesus, but the formation is different for every believer. The foundation should not be confused with the formation. One comes first, and then the other. One is the same, and the other is different.

When Christian disciplers don't understand the difference between foundational and formational discipleship, it's easy to build Christians turned backward.

Oops!

About the same time, I thought of foundational discipleship in Matthew 7, and having heard the story of the house facing the wrong direction, I saw a local church booklet entitled *A New Believer's Journey to Maturity*.

The contents were baptism, tithing, the evil of denominationalism, a year-long Bible reading plan, why the gifts of the Spirit were only for the first century, and how Baptists and Presbyterians taught false doctrine.

Is this a good foundation?

A wise builder has the correct and best materials in a foundation. To disciple correctly, we must understand what should be included in foundational and formational discipleship.

A great foundation must follow the architect's blueprint.

This is LampPost Rule #3: Understand the blueprint.

600 Pastors

Years back, I had a discussion with a top leader in a ministry that has won more people to the Lord than perhaps any other ministry in Christian history.

I asked what their ministry did about foundational discipleship. He didn't understand my reference to "foundational discipleship," as he mentioned that they left discipleship up to the local churches in the countries in which they worked.

I then asked the ministry leader if he could give an example of successful discipleship that happened after their ministry left an area.

He cited a denomination in the Philippines that was having success with discipleship.

Perhaps I should have told him (but I didn't) that two months earlier, I had been in the Philippines leading a conference of 600 pastors from the denomination that he had just mentioned.

At the beginning of the conference, I asked those 600 pastors the following questions:

Knowing that most new believers walk away from faithfulness in the first three months, if I gave you a new believer, would you know exactly what to do—best practices—for discipling this new believer in the first three months?

I'm sure all of you would know something, but would you know the best practices of discipleship that would be most effective for a new believer in the first three months?

Out of the 600 pastors and church leaders, only fifteen raised their hands.

Foundational and Formational Discipleship

Foundational discipleship happens in the first three months of a new believer's walk with Jesus. What comes later—one year, two years, or forty years later—must be built upon this foundation.

What comes later is formational discipleship. The foundation is the same for all believers, but the formation is different.

When an author, scholar, or pastor says that there are many approaches to discipleship, they haven't accounted for foundational discipleship. All believers have the same foundation.

But all followers also have a different formation. The "many approaches" philosophy relates to formational and not foundational discipleship. We will talk about the difference between foundation and formational discipleship throughout this book.

But let's review:

Foundational discipleship: the same for all believers and important in the first three months.

Formational discipleship: different for all believers and occurring after the first three months.

A high percentage of discipleship materials produced today are more formational than foundational. And with the foundation needed first, formational discipleship isn't effective with new believers.

The Blueprint for Foundational Discipleship

As a new pastor who mostly discipled new believers in the first years of my ministry, I made two observations. These observations vastly improved my effectiveness in disciplemaking.

First, there are four foundational disciplines of the Christian faith.

Second, all new believers experience the same temptations.

I saw that all new believers needed the same foundational disciplines and that all new believers had the same temptations. Foundational discipleship must build upon an understanding of these foundational disciplines and enable the followers of Jesus to ward off their similar temptations.

Four Foundational Disciplines

As I worked with hundreds of new believers, I noticed that those who spent time reading the Bible, praying, being involved with fellowship, and discipling others matured quickly in Christ, while those who didn't walked away from faithfulness.

I began calling these four practices the "foundational disciplines" of the Christian faith.

No, Jesus doesn't say in Matthew 28:21–22, "The four basic disciplines of the Christian faith are prayer, Bible, fellowship, and discipleship." (Those quick with their Bible knowledge realize that verses 21 and 22 do not exist in Matthew 28.)

The Apostle Paul doesn't give a list of the four basic disciplines in his epistles. Neither do any of the other Biblical authors.

But Jesus, Paul, and all of Scripture provide a significant amount of content extolling the need for Bible, prayer, fellowship, and discipleship. I doubt anyone would debate the elementary importance of these four practices.

I have focused on these four disciplines as essential in the right foundation of believers for the last fifty years. But learning these disciplines can become a dry religion without an undergirding relationship with Jesus.

Bible, prayer, fellowship, and discipleship should be motivated by a love for Jesus. The four foundational disciplines of the Christian faith are experienced relationally through the *Principle of Specificity*.

1. Specificity and Prayer

Specific prayers are the foundation of praying. Jesus taught that we have an "ask and receive" relationship with Him (Matthew 7:7). When we receive an answer to specific prayers, we know that our Father in heaven loves and cares for us.

In foundational discipleship (see the book *First Steps Conversations,* Session Five[8]), we ask disciples to write down a specific request. We frame this teaching by saying, "If you could have one prayer request answered—guaranteed—what would it be?"

Amazingly, the request is often answered. When God answers prayers, especially for a new believer, the relationship becomes real. Initial answered prayers with a new believer set a great foundation for growing in faith.

2. Specificity and the Bible

Every new believer has a specific sin to struggle against in following Jesus. This stumbling point will cause many to walk away from faithfulness.

The book of James gives the solution:

> *Get rid of all the filth and evil in your lives, and humbly accept the word God has planted in your hearts, for it has the power to save your souls.* (James 1:21, NLT)

The specific sin is a "life issue," and the antidote verse of Scripture is a "life verse."

This struggle with a particular sin can last a long time, even through their entire walk with Jesus. However, they don't have to stumble in major defeat, especially if life verses have been memorized.

One day, while I was teaching the *Principle of Specificity* with Bible verses in a correctional institution, a large inmate stood up. Perhaps you will notice the humor in this situation when I say—he was large and in prison for murder.

I was locked in a room with this man. There were no guards and no place for me to run. After the inmate stood, he stared at me and said flatly, "I have an anger problem."

Immediately, I thought, *I hope my guardian angel is on duty today.*

Then he said, "But this is the first time I have confessed that I have an anger problem. And I've memorized my life verse on forgiveness. For the first time, I am experiencing peace."

Can you imagine the reduction in the crime rate if all prisoners could identify life issues and memorize life verses?

3. Specificity and Fellowship

God created the church made of specific people with specific gifts that are used in specific ministries.

> *God has given each of you a gift from his great variety of spiritual gifts. Use them well to serve one another.* (1 Peter 4:11, NLT)

New believers (and older believers, too) must learn to fit their spiritual gifts into the body of Christ. How we serve creates our narrow path for following Christ. Nobody else can serve like us, nobody else has our gift mix, and God empowers our ministries using the gifts that He has given to us.

Consider a puzzle.

Each member of a local church has a specific piece of this puzzle. Striving for unity, each church member must lay down their piece so that the total picture of the church's calling can be visibly understood.

How blessed it is for the church to dwell in unity.

4. Specificity and Disciplemaking

When we disciple believers, we know that we are obedient to the Great Commission.

> **When we disciple believers, we know we are obedient to the Great Commission.**

I believe that God has specific followers of Jesus that we are to disciple.

It goes like this:

We encounter a believer, and during our conversation, we ask this question: "Have you been discipled?" The answer is almost always "no," even if the follower has spent years in the church because few Christians have been in a one-to-one discipling relationship.

Then we ask, "Would you enjoy going through a one-to-one, three-month discipleship plan that will help you build or renew the foundation of your faith?"

The answer is almost always, "Yes!"

Jesus said in John 4:35 that the fields are white for the harvest, and as workers in this harvest through disciplemaking, we will experience the blessing of God using us.

Just like the Bible doesn't list four foundational disciplines, the word "specificity" can't be found in Scripture either. However, the four foundational disciplines of the Christian faith are activated by the faith gained by practicing the *Principle of Specificity*.

The *Principle of Specificity* elevates mere disciplines into a loving relationship with Jesus.

Similar Temptations

Observing hundreds of new believers, I noticed many asked the same questions and went through the same temptations.

This should not be surprising, as physical newborn babies have similar developmental areas, while those "born again" also have similar spiritual growth issues. Infant development is the same for babies throughout the world, and newborn Christians have the same areas in which to grow, whether Filipino, American, or Italian.

All believers have the same foundational growth areas.

Paul writes:

> *But I, brothers, could not address you as spiritual people, but as people of the flesh, as infants in Christ. I fed you with milk, not solid food, for you were not ready for it. And even now you are not yet ready.* (1 Corinthians 3:1–2, ESV)

What are the four same or similar temptations for new believers?

As I discipled and helped new believers mature in Christ, I constantly heard the following questions and temptations.

1. Doubts and Discouragement

After a new believer accepts Jesus, there can be "buyer's remorse." Those of us who have purchased a house understand this doubt when we wake up the first morning after closing on the mortgage, thinking, "Uh-oh, I have to make payments on this house for thirty years."

A new follower might ask:

Is my living arrangement with this person scriptural?
What will my friends think?
Is the Bible true? My friend said it was filled with myths.

If doubt persists, it can lead to a *moment of discouragement*, in which new believers suddenly give up and walk away from faithfulness. The best solution is a one-to-one discipling relationship of encouragement.

I tell my disciples, "When you get discouraged, please call me."

2. Saying "No" to Temptations

I had just memorized Romans 13:14:

> *But put on the Lord Jesus Christ and make no provision for the flesh in regard to its lusts.* (NASB1995)

I was nineteen and walking through our local mall on a hot spring day, and I saw a scantily clad young woman. My mind began to wander from beauty to lust and just then—*boom!*—that verse popped into my mind:

> *But put on the Lord Jesus Christ and make no provision for the flesh in regard to its lusts.*

I remember thinking, "Memorizing Scripture has ruined my lust life." I then realized the power of the Spirit using Scripture. All new believers must learn to say "no" to specific temptations, and it can be defeated, as the book of James teaches:

> *Therefore put away all filthiness and rampant wickedness and receive with meekness the implanted word, which is able to save your souls.* (James 1:21, ESV)

3. Knowing the Right Priorities

New followers of Jesus are now serving God's Kingdom and not their personal kingdom. Priorities must be changed. They need to become a Big Kingdom disciple and move away from serving the kingdom of self.

Another verse I memorized as a new follower of Jesus was:

> *But seek first His kingdom and His righteousness and all things shall be added to you.* (Matthew 6:33, NASB1995)

I was offered a job soon after I began leading my band of Jesus Freaks.

A friend offered me a job at the local YMCA. He had heard about my growing influence on the youth in our community. He asked me to visit him in his office and said, "Grant, you have no organization behind what you are doing. I have an opening here at the YMCA. You can have this job, and, in the future, with the right education and training, I believe you will go far in this organization."

It was a great offer, especially the salary that would come with the job, as at that time, I was living by faith (no earned income).

But I declined. I believed that seeking His Kingdom first meant continuing the ministry to which God had called me.

4. Understanding God's Will

A new believer will soon have to make specific decisions about their lives. This college or that college, this job, how about living in this area of the country, relationships, and businesses—all have the specific request of, "Is this God's will?"

Discipleship must include knowing how to find God's will. And the skill must be learned soon after conversion. Life decisions enhance or distract from faithfulness to Jesus.

With the right instructions, a new believer will say, "I know I made the right choice. I prayed about it, studied the Bible, listened to the Spirit within me, and asked for wisdom from others. And God has blessed my decision."

A House Facing the Right Direction

What is the content of great discipleship?

As disciplers, we aren't building the Taj Mahal or the Empire State Building. We don't need a degree in architecture, as the correct foundation is simply defined and can be built by any follower of Jesus.

We just need to look at the blueprint a few times, knowing that foundational discipleship has four disciplines to be developed by all Christians and that all new believers go through similar temptations.

If we practice foundational and not formational discipleship with new believers, we will build houses facing the right direction.

There are four principles or best practices for foundational discipleship, which we will discuss in the next chapter.

Chapter 3: Read the Blueprint!

Review:
- LampPost Rule #1: Admit the problem.
- LampPost Rule #2: Know the right definition and content.
- LampPost Rule #3: Understand the blueprint.

Interlude #3 illustrates the difference between formational and foundational discipleship.

Interlude #3:

Two Houses

Below are two houses with the same foundation but with different formations.

Foundation
Same for all houses and the same for all believers

Formation
Different for all houses and different for all believers

If someone says that discipleship is *different* for all believers, they are half-right and half-wrong, as the foundation is the same for all believers.

If someone says that discipleship is the *same* for all believers, they are half-right and half-wrong, as the formation of all believers is different.

Believers have the same foundation but a different formation!

Chapter 4:

Things Ya Do and Things Ya Don't Do!

Jesus is looking for help, for he cannot do the work alone. Who will come forward to help him and work with him?[9]

A favorite passage of mine for disciplemaking is found in the book of Hebrews:

> *For though by this time you ought to be teachers, you need someone to teach you again the basic principles of the oracles of God. You need milk, not solid food, for everyone who lives on milk is unskilled in the word of righteousness, since he is a child. But solid food is for the mature, for those who have their powers of discernment trained by constant practice to distinguish good from evil.*
> (Hebrews 5:12–14, ESV)

The author of Hebrews discusses correct building practices with disciplemaking.

Words and phrases like *basic principles, milk, unskilled, solid food, maturity, powers of discernment,* and *trained by constant practice* are helpful when discussing how to make disciples.

I've focused on "trained by constant practice" in this book. I'm writing what I've found works and doesn't work in the over fifty years I've been making disciples who disciple others.

In the last chapter, we discussed foundational and formational discipleship.

To best understand foundational discipleship, think, "Same!" To best understand formational discipleship, think, "Different!" Foundational discipleship is the same for everyone, while formational discipleship is different for everyone.

A significant percentage of current discipleship material is a mishmash of both foundational and formational material and practices.

All discipleship is good, but blending foundational and formational will dilute efforts to turn the 80 percent walk-away rate of new believers in the first three months into the victory of 80 percent still involved in a local church three years later.

To become a skilled disciplemaker, we must understand the content of four basic disciplines and four similar temptations in foundational discipleship (explained in Chapter 3).

Then, we need to know the best practices to become skilled in disciplemaking.

A Foundational Conversation

My wife and I were blessed to be able to build a house for our family.

The foundation came first.

We dug a deep hole for the foundation and basement, which quickly filled with water. This caused major anxiety on my part, as money had been spent purchasing a lot, clearing trees, grading, and digging a large hole.

The general contractor wasn't concerned. He said, "I have a guy who can get rid of the water and build you a great foundation."

A few days later, the "foundation guy" showed up. He was an older gentleman, and he was wearing a suit and tie. I didn't know what to make of him. His crusty attitude and salty words further undermined my confidence.

I remember our first conversation.

Me: "Hi, I'm Grant Edwards."

He responded: "I'm da guy to put da blocks for de basement. #$%^&!@ Dis ho'le dis filt wi wader."

Me: "Is that a problem?"

He responded: "Nah, ben doin dis for 40 yers. Don't wory!"

Me: "How are you going to get rid of the water and get me a foundation on which I can build a house?"

He responded: "Wel, der r things ya do and der r things ya don't do!"

I was praying at that moment that he knew those things!
And he did. While laying blocks in his suit and tie, he put in a cement block foundation that has been dry for twenty-five years.

Best Practices of Foundational Discipleship

Foundational Christianity isn't rocket science.

It's the four foundational disciplines of prayer, Bible, fellowship, and discipleship. Also, there are four similar temptations that all new believers experience—overcoming doubt, dealing with temptation, discovering the right priorities, and discerning God's will.

But once we have the basics or the foundation of discipleship, there are best practices or things that you do and things that you don't do.

LampPost Rule #4: Know best practices.

Let's first consider that *der r things ya do,* and then let's think about *der r things ya don't do!*

Some Things Ya Do!

The first thing to do: It's one-to-one!

Let me note that all discipleship, no matter if it is foundational or not, is better than no discipleship. But a friend recently said, "I can summarize the discipleship practices of most churches in two words."

Intrigued, I responded, "And the two words would be?"

He said, "Come back!"

He then went on to say, "Every teaching in the New Testament that refers to discipleship, or infers discipleship, isn't distant but "close-in" relationships. I'm unsure how you can consider discipleship as returning to a church building or attending a small group."

The New Testament indicates three types of relationships—large group, small group, and one-to-one relationships.

Worship and preaching work best in a large group assembly. Encouragement and ministering to the needs of followers work best in small groups. However, personal change, along with confession and speaking the truth in love, work best in one-to-one relationships.

The words "one another" are found about 100 times in the New Testament.

The Greek word for "one another" is a reciprocal pronoun indicating that when you pray for one another (James 5:16), there should be another person. If we serve one another, there should be another person (Galatians 5:13)!

The "one another" verses instruct us to:

- Be devoted to one another (Romans 12:19)
- Accept one another (Romans 15:7)
- Admonish one another (Romans 15:14)
- Have concern for one another (1 Corinthians 12:15)
- Encourage one another (1 Thessalonians 5:11)

And many more! Foundational discipleship is "one another" at its best.

The second thing to do: The first three months!

Why are the first ninety days important?

I love reading books about business. The most helpful and successful business books tend to reflect truth already found in the Bible. These books teach principles based on research involving time and money that I've never been able to afford.

When I make a conclusion in this book, such as *80 percent walk away from faithfulness in the first three months*, my evidence is more anecdotal (perhaps you've noticed). The qualitative evidence that I present often comes from statistical analysis found in business books.

With my anecdotes and best business practices in mind, let's consider a book published in 2003 entitled *The First 90 Days*. This book was a runaway bestseller for over ten years, selling over eight hundred thousand copies in English and translated into twenty-seven languages.

The title indicates the content—*The First 90 Days!*

A quote from the 2013 version gives a good reason for ninety days:

> *Your goal in every transition is to get as rapidly as possible to the break-even point. This is the point at which you have contributed as much value to your new organization as you have consumed from it.*[10]

The idea of "onboarding" new employees was catapulted by this book.

The question asked and answered in this book was how to get employees from consuming company resources during their initial hiring to a break-even point when the employees' efforts contributed as much value to the company as the resources consumed by them from the company.

The book teaches how to get to this break-even point in ninety days.

The book's research questioned 1,300 business leaders about transitions from one position to another position in a company:

"Transitions into new roles are the most challenging times in the professional lives of leaders." And nearly three-quarters agreed that *"success or failure during the first few months is a strong predictor of overall success or failure in the job."* So even though a bad transition does not necessarily doom you to failure, it makes success a lot less likely.[11]

If 80 percent of those who accept Jesus walk away from faithfulness within three months of accepting Jesus, then significant resources of churches in all countries should focus on this one problem.

The first ninety days!

As mentioned previously in Chapter 1, the church has never had difficulty with reaching the lost, but most churches have difficulty keeping the saved. About this, Jesus said:

> **The church has never had difficulty reaching the lost, but keeping the saved.**

The harvest is plentiful, but the laborers are few. Therefore, pray earnestly to the Lord of the harvest to send out laborers into His harvest. (Luke 10:2, ESV)

Discussions on discipleship abound today. The church is awakening to the need for workers in the harvest. There are blogs, vlogs, books, podcasts, and conferences on discipleship.

My concern is that most of the discussion about discipleship is irrelevant to new believers in the first three months.

The third thing to do: Focus on a conversation!

For over fifty years, I've been having conversations with new believers.

My disciplemaking technique is having a conversation, not a classroom approach, and not just reading and discussing a book in a coffee shop. When I began disciplemaking, I would learn something and talk about it to those around me.

I found that one of the most important aspects of discipling is simply having a conversation.

I tell those I'm training to disciple, "If you can have a conversation, you can disciple."

This isn't a rambling conversation about any topic. I've developed ten lessons (published as *First Steps Conversations*, found at GrantEdwardsAuthor.com), where a discipler sits with a new believer and reads the material back and forth.

> **If you can have a conversation, you can disciple.**

A sort of a conversational script is needed to keep the conversation focused on the foundational disciplines and similar temptations. And a conversation rooted in Scripture will be empowered or enlightened by the presence of the Spirit.

A great discipleship combination—discipler, disciple, and Holy Spirit—is a powerful formula for maturing in Christ.

In 1975, I was discussing prayer with a new believer. The verse that we were talking about was:

> *Ask, and it will be given to you; seek, and you will find; knock, and it will be opened to you. For everyone who asks receives, and the one who seeks finds, and to the one who knocks it will be opened. Or which one of you, if his son asks him for bread, will give him a stone? Or if he asks for a fish, will give him a serpent? If you then, who are evil, know how to give good gifts to your children, how much more will your Father who is in heaven give good things to those who ask him!* (Matthew 7:7–11, ESV)

After reading this verse, my disciple said, "I need $100 to pay for my gas bill."

I had been discipling new believers for several years and noticed that many of them took this verse at face value.

He then said, "If Jesus said to ask for a fish or a loaf 2,000 years ago, certainly He wouldn't mind if I asked for money to pay my gas bill."

I backpedaled, thinking that prayer was more, "God bless me" rather than being so bold as to ask for something specific.

But pray we did, and answer God did.

Fifty years ago, this was a moment when Jesus jumped off the pages of Scripture into an actual prayer request—a specific request. My disciple and I would know if Jesus answered or didn't answer the request.

I was ready to defend Jesus when my disciple didn't get the money to pay his bill. But I didn't need to, as my disciple went home that evening and opened a letter from his grandmother containing one hundred dollars.

From a simple conversation, I learned the principle of asking specifically. Prayer became a relational connection with God, not just a foundational discipline.

I still teach this lesson of specificity—of asking specific requests when disciplemaking.

Conversations allow Scripture to become active and alive. When believers discuss, the Spirit then instructs, teaches, and encourages. God becomes real. The new follower senses God's presence, and this relationship changes everything.

As a disciple develops a close relationship with Jesus, trust in this relationship enables strength and perseverance. The deep roots of relational faith foundationally allow new believers to withstand their future storms. They know Jesus listens and answers in any circumstance.

And they learn to make bold and specific requests!

The fourth thing to do: Be an example!

The Apostle Paul wrote:

> *Follow my example as I follow the example of Christ.*
> (1 Corinthians 11:1, NIV)

When I first began discipling, we were a bunch of ex-hippies living in a Jesus House. (Definition of a Jesus House: an old house needing many repairs where a bunch of hippies live together who have recently accepted Jesus as Lord and Savior.)

I was the leader. More and more ex-hippies (we called ourselves "Jesus Freaks") kept getting saved and showing up to learn about Jesus.

It was difficult to talk about prayer without setting the example of praying. My inconsistency would be noticed by those living in the Jesus House with me. If I asked everyone to read their Bible and yet did not read my Bible, nobody would listen to me.

How could I discuss having fellowship without learning forgiveness?

Discipleship required an example.

When I encouraged those living in the Jesus House to disciple, I was learning to disciple at the same time. I didn't know a lot about discipling, but I was discipling, and I found that discipling is the best way of learning how to disciple.

We were learning discipleship together. But I was setting an example!

Somehow, it worked!

My discipling was authentic. When I stumbled with impure thoughts and meditated on Scripture to find freedom, I helped others find victory in the same manner. I didn't have an office lined with books or, at that time, a seminary degree.

I walked with Jesus, I learned how to follow Him, and then I discipled others. Those that I discipled then discipled others.

And we stopped losing 80 percent of those who had accepted Jesus as Savior.

Some Things Ya Don't Do!

My "foundation guy" that I mentioned at the beginning of this chapter did such a great job with the foundation and basement of my house that I hired him to put up a brick chimney.

It's a tall chimney.

When he quoted me the price of the chimney, it was more than I expected. I also noticed that the chimney's height was about fifteen feet above my roof line. Now I knew why the price seemed too much.

So I asked: "Why don't you lower the height so I can save some money?"

His initial response was: "*%^#@*%!"

Then he said: "Naw, tha don't wrk. Da chmney neds t'be tallert den da top of da roof, or in de high wnd, da smok wilt blow down da chmney into yer house."

I was glad "de guy building my chmney" had forty years of experience doing brickwork.

Let's all remember my foundation guy's advice when it comes to discipling, "Der r things ya do and der r things ya don't do!"

The first thing not to do: Write your own discipleship material!

There are about 1,200 current titles on the topic of discipleship listed on Amazon. The number of books increases continually, and this book is probably 1,201!

I've purchased several of these books, as I like to keep up with best practices. But a high percentage of these books are written by authors who haven't had enough practice with disciplemaking.

Is ten discipled enough? How about twenty? How about hundreds? While reading the discipleship plans in some of these books, I think:

- Thirty-six lessons are too long for foundational discipleship.
- Why did I just read about the creation story and the flood for a new follower of Jesus?
- Lots of rules and rigid practices, but no developing a relationship with Jesus.

I often wonder while reading, "Has this author ever discipled anyone?" It sounds like me telling my foundation guy how to build a chimney.

The second thing not to do: Make small groups the primary place for initial discipleship.

Small groups are great.

In the church that I pastored, we began small groups in the mid-70s. A three-month one-to-one discipling relationship needed a handoff to a small group for continued spiritual maturity.

I cringe at a conference when someone tells me that they are going to use my book *First Steps Conversations* with the small groups in their church. I know it will be just another book to study, then placed on a shelf afterward.

The purpose of disciplemaking is to make disciples who make disciples . . . and studying a book in a small group won't have the impetus to support a culture of everyone discipling one-to-one.

Despite most churches already having small groups, the number of disciplemaking-producing churches in America is about five percent.[12] Small groups help with formational discipleship but fail with one-to-one foundational discipleship.

The third thing not to do: Treat disciplemaking as another program in a church.

Disciplemaking as just another church program, among many other programs, won't work. Listing discipleship on a website next to the children's ministry, the prayer team ministry or the hospitality ministry isn't sufficient.

Discipleship must become the vision and culture of a local church that undergirds every other church ministry, program, or mission!

This book is about a concept called *The LampPost Strategy*.

Throughout the rest of this book, I will describe *The LampPost Strategy for Disciplemaking*. This is *discipleship that works!*

In the next chapter, let's build confidence in our ability to become a discipler. Now let's say . . .

"I can do this!"

Review:

- LampPost Rule #1: Admit the problem.
- LampPost Rule #2: Know the right definition and content.
- LampPost Rule #3: Understand the blueprint.
- LampPost Rule #4: Know best practices.

Before reading Chapter 5, find out more about a conversational script in *Interlude #4*.

Interlude #4:

Seinfeld and Conversational Script

The book I wrote for foundational discipleship is entitled *First Steps Conversations*.

It is written as a conversation that the Spirit joins for conviction and discernment.

Books aren't written to be read aloud, but scripts must be read out loud. I use "conversational script" in *First Steps Conversations*—the discipler and the disciple reading back and forth.

On YouTube®, you can watch *Seinfeld* table reads, where the cast prepares for a show by sitting around a table reading the script, with writers and producers in chairs behind them reading scene headings and stage directions and the cast reading the dialogue.

And everyone laughs.

While developing my idea of "conversational script," I watched too many of these videos. What fascinated me was that a boring script became funny during the table read.

Jokes and other comments are added spontaneously by actors. Dialogue on the page works, or it doesn't. Writers and editors listen during the read and take notes to update the script.

Before I get lost in the script writing process for *Seinfeld*, I need to emphasize a point—at a table read, the script comes alive as the actors read it. I was drawn into watching the YouTube® videos of *Seinfeld* table reads because they were authentic and fun.

The technique of "conversational script" works well when a discipler and a disciple sit at a table and read the content. Discipleship should be a table read discussion—back and forth with the Spirit revealing insight through the conversation.

A discipler and a disciple can read a script, no matter their maturity. New disciples can disciple new disciples; mature disciples can disciple mature disciples; and yes, new disciples can disciple mature disciplers who haven't been discipled.

Just read the script and let the Spirit take charge!

Chapter 5:

I Can Do This!

Let us not lose heart in doing good, for in due time we will reap if we do not grow weary. (Galatians 6:9, ESV)

I became a Christian and pastor at the same time.

After deciding at age 10 to turn away from my faith, on New Year's Eve 1971/1972, I returned to following Jesus on Daytona Beach. Two weeks later, I led sixteen of my friends to receive Jesus as their Lord.

Admittedly, becoming a pastor and a Christian in the same time frame isn't the typical calling/training pattern of most pastors. However, this on-the-job education gave me a unique perspective on how to approach discipleship. I didn't have to report to a denominational supervisor, I wasn't overly influenced by seminary professors, and few Christian authors were writing on the topic.

I learned disciplemaking myself.

The Jesus Movement revival was messy. Those who became believers and leaders in this revival often didn't fit into older forms of Christian tradition and culture.

Finding myself alone in my search for effective disciplemaking while at the same time being the organizational leader in a ministry of ex-hippies who inherently didn't want to be organized resulted in a lot of frustration and discouragement for me.

I was overwhelmed and knew I needed help.

Older adults from the church in which I grew up as a child began showing an interest in The One Way House (we named our ministry and building after John's description of Jesus as the only way to God—see John 14:6). So I discussed attending this church with "our group," and we decided to give it a try.

The following Sunday, about forty of us walked into this church.

We came early and found the sanctuary empty, so we sat in the first four rows. We were quickly noticed by the regulars as they arrived. There couldn't have been a greater contrast of attendees in any church in America on that Sunday.

In the first four rows, we had tie-dye; in the other pews, there were dresses and polyester suits. In the first four rows, there was long, stringy hair, and in the rest of the pews sat crew cuts and hair-sprayed hair. In the first four rows, wafting from unwashed blue jeans of those new to our ministry, we had the residue of various types of smoke, which didn't mix well with the perfume and aftershave lotion in the other pews.

The church organist began playing and no one started singing.

We didn't know the songs, and everyone else was too busy staring at us to respond to the opening refrains from the organ.

Somehow, everyone managed that first week and the next and the next. But there were some difficulties and questions like:

> *Why can't they dress up for God's house?*
> *Have they stopped smoking dope and having premarital sex?*
> *Are Catholics attending with them?*

I could have handled the starkly different sense of style and the challenging questions, but I was increasingly discouraged by the realization that we just weren't wanted.

I was ready to stop attending.

On the fourth Sunday, after the service, an older lady with white hair approached me. As I was talking to some of my friends, I could see her coming out of the corner of my eye. She had a stern look on her face and was carrying a large wood-handled umbrella.

"Uh, oh!" I thought, "I'm either going to get a tongue-lashing, an umbrella-thrashing, or both."

Instead, Doris Cox came close to me and grabbed my hand, saying, "I love what you are doing, and don't get discouraged. Keep doing what you are doing. You are the only one who can do this."

With all the stories and anecdotes shared in this book, I only mention one name—Doris Cox! I give her honor because of the needed cross-cultural encouragement she gave me that day.

My attitude of "I can do this" and not quitting or giving up because of disillusionment started that morning with an older sister's stern face and large umbrella.

Thank you, Mrs. Cox!

The LampPost Rule #5: I can do this!

Having come to an understanding that I needed to disciple new believers and that we should attend a church, I asked the question, "How can a lot of new believers be discipled in this ministry?"

I wished the Apostle Paul had written two epistles entitled "First and Second Disciplemaking," but he didn't, and I realize now that God uses His saints throughout church history to develop both theoretical and practical theology.

It's not easy figuring out disciplemaking.

I made a lot of mistakes early in my ministry with disciplemaking, and I still do. Fortunately, many of my mistakes have led to helpful insights for best practices.

One of the early mistakes that I made was trying to disciple everyone myself. In my ministry, everyone was a new believer, and I thought their "newness" of faith disqualified them from discipling.

Quickly becoming overburdened, I realized one day, "Hey, there's nothing wrong with new believers making disciples. I am a new believer myself."

Duh! It's amazing how insights come from necessity.

I also read Matthew 9.

I noticed that Jesus had difficulty with crowds too. As I read this chapter, I thought, *Okay, Jesus, what are you going to do about the "too many people" problem?*

I wanted to know His solution, so I read chapter 9 several times to find out.

Jesus raised the daughter of a synagogue official from the dead. A woman who had been suffering from a hemorrhage for twelve years touched the fringe of His cloak and was instantly healed.

Matthew 9 reports, *"The news spread throughout all the land."*

Then two blind men were healed, a mute, demon-possessed man was delivered, and finally, this happened:

> *And Jesus went throughout all the cities and villages, teaching in their synagogues and proclaiming the gospel of the kingdom, and healing every disease and every affliction. When he saw the crowds, he had compassion for them because they were harassed and helpless, like sheep without a shepherd. Then he said to his disciples, "The harvest is plentiful, but the laborers are few."* (vv. 35–37, ESV)

What did Jesus do with crowds? He didn't stop His ministry, but He did say to his disciples:

> *Ask the Lord of the harvest to send out workers into his harvest-ready fields.* (v. 38, ESV)

Jesus wasn't going to disciple all those following Him. He had another idea. Matthew chapter 10 continues with Jesus' solution for the "too many people" problem.

> *[Jesus] called his twelve disciples and gave them authority over unclean spirits, to cast them out, and to heal every kind of disease and sickness.* (Matthew 10:1, ESV)

Luke 10 then describes how Jesus expanded from his discipleship ministry of twelve to seventy-two:

> *After this the Lord appointed seventy-two others and sent them on ahead of him two by two into every town and place where he himself was about to go. He said to them, "The harvest is plentiful, but the workers are few. Therefore ask the Lord of the harvest to send out workers into his harvest.* (Luke 10:1–2, ESV)

Jesus solved His crowd problem by sending workers into the harvest. Most of these workers had to be relatively new to the faith. If releasing new believers into the harvest was good enough for Jesus, it was good enough for me, too!

I then began teaching that everyone could be a worker in the harvest—that all believers could disciple—no matter how mature they were in following Jesus or how long they had been following Him.

I found that disciplemakers matured deeply and that those who didn't disciple stopped growing spiritually.

As I've studied and practiced discipleship over the past five decades, I've seen programs and teachings flounder that didn't promote, train, or develop new believers as disciplemakers. I've noticed, too, that the best disciplers are those who started discipling at the beginning of their walk with Jesus.

New believers should have disciplemaking as their initial spiritual DNA.

As disciplemaking became the focus of The One Way House in the '70s, I received pushback and criticism. Some believers from "my new church" began attending, and with the news of the large crowds at our ministry, believers from other churches visited.

> **New believers should have disciplemaking as their initial spiritual DNA.**

Many of these believers were ten, twenty, or even forty years past their confession of faith, and none of them were disciplemakers! In fact, I quickly discerned that many of these "church folks" needed to be discipled!

Noticing the crowds, one pastor said, "You have to stop reaching young people for Jesus; you don't have any room in your meeting space."

We didn't stop evangelism, but we trained everyone to disciple following the example of Jesus, who sent out twelve and then seventy-two.

There were other lessons that I learned about the undergirding culture of discipleship.

If you turned to ABC's *Wide World of Sports* from 1971 onward, you would see a ski jumper fall and flail during an attempted jump, with announcer Jim McKay saying in the background, "The thrill of victory and the agony of defeat."

Next are a few "thrill and agony" lessons I learned from my flailing, failing, and eventual success as a disciplemaker.

Thrill and Agony Lessons

My four "thrill and agony" lessons that led me to embrace my "you can do it" view of discipleship are:

- I can disciple! We should all disciple!
- Define and confine discipleship.
- Sharing testimonies.
- No greater feeling than God working through us!

I can disciple! We should all disciple!

When I say, "I can disciple," I add, "We should all disciple!"

A discipler matures faster and has a deeper relationship with Jesus than those who don't disciple. Jesus was talking to relatively new believers when He said:

> *By this my Father is glorified, that you bear much fruit and so prove to be my disciples.* (John 15:8, ESV)

I was approached early in my discipling years by a significant pastor in our community. He wanted to know what we were doing to help new believers mature in Christ. He was surprised when I told him that all believers should disciple no matter their experience or depth of faith as a believer.

He told me, "Only mature Christians can disciple, and it's best to have a seminary degree."

I responded, "These are brand new believers. I've observed that many of them walk away from Jesus very quickly. Would you be willing to disciple some of them?"

No, he didn't want to disciple or help. I knew that he didn't have a clue about disciplemaking, especially with Jesus Freaks. I thought, but didn't tell him, *I would rather do what I'm doing wrong than what you are not doing at all.*

A few weeks after my discussion with the significant pastor, I drove up the driveway to our ministry building and noticed a sister standing in front of five new believers who were all sitting on the porch steps. She was reading my discipleship material to them and even pointing her finger at them for emphasis.

I know this broke the one-to-one rule of disciplemaking, but the rule wasn't firmly established at that time.

This finger-pointing discipler later became a professor at one of the most influential universities in America and is still walking with Jesus. And every one of those disciples, having endured "finger-pointing" discipleship, are still following Christ.

Define and Confine Discipleship

If every believer disciples, especially new believers, they can't all be released to do their own thing. It would be chaos, with each believer serving up personal opinions of disciplemaking.

Discipleship must be defined exactly as what is said during the foundational discipleship process, and the one-to-one discipleship relationship must be confined to only three months.

If the content of initial discipleship focuses on the basic foundational disciplines and similar temptations of new believers—and that content is published and easy to use—all believers can disciple using the same material.

Then, a church pastor doesn't need to worry about what is being taught in the discipling process of a church.

Obviously, those who have discipled will develop better techniques and more testimonies of disciplemaking, but it is amazing that new believers, even without years of experience, are very effective.

The enthusiasm of a new believer makes up for what is lacking in experience. And if the content used in discipleship maintains solid foundational practices, the young discipler can't wander into opinions or express immature beliefs.

The discipling relationship must also be confined.

> It's essential that the discipler/disciple relationship becomes a co-worker relationship after three months.

Spiritual and emotional codependency issues begin to surface if a discipling relationship continues for too long. It's essential that the identified discipler/disciple relationship becomes a co-worker relationship of equals after three months.

While foundational discipleship is one-to-one, lasting three months, formational discipleship includes mentors, counselors, and tutors and can be long-term. Counselors and mentors in long-term relationships are trained to avoid codependency issues in longer-lasting formational discipleship.

In the 1970s and 1980s, a few Jesus Movement ministries sprang up promoting discipleship. I visited a well-known Jesus House that was founded for discipleship and even had a book published about its history.

Hoping to learn more about discipleship, I visited the ministry with a friend.

The ministry was hospitable. When my friend and I knocked on the door unannounced, we were greeted and offered a place to sleep for the night. Hippies to Jesus Freaks were mobile, often hitching across the country at any seeming whim of the Spirit.

There were plenty of places to crash; just find a Jesus House.

We had a great time of fellowship and discussed discipleship at the ministry. But I also had a sense of unease. To me, it seemed like everyone talked too much about the leader of that ministry and about the person who was their discipler.

In one conversation, a young man said to me, "I'm thinking of purchasing a car, but I have to ask my discipler first."

Alarm bells!

Foundational discipleship should never result in control. Discussion brings wisdom, of course, but foundational disciplemaking is about freedom in Jesus and not placing believers in positions of submission to their disciplers.

Sharing Testimonies

Sharing testimonies became an essential part of my disciplemaking.

Prayer, Bible reading, fellowship, and discipleship are the four foundational disciplines of the Christian faith. They move believers from theory to experience and finally to a fuller relationship with Jesus through testimony.

We believe that God answers prayer. We know that Jesus gives spectacular promises of His willingness to answer prayers.

> *Whatever you ask in my name, this I will do, that the Father may be glorified in the Son.* (John 14:13, ESV)
>
> *Ask, and it will be given to you; seek, and you will find; knock, and it will be opened to you. For everyone who asks receives, and the one who seeks finds, and to the one who knocks it will be opened. Or which one of you, if his son asks him for bread, will give him a stone? Or if he asks for a fish, will give him a serpent? If you then, who are*

> *evil, know how to give good gifts to your children, how much more will your Father who is in heaven give good things to those who ask him!* (Matthew 7:7–11, ESV)

But promises in Scripture become real when Jesus answers a specific prayer. The experience of God answering a prayer undergirds a trust upon which to grow a relationship with the Father in heaven.

I encourage those I'm discipling to make specific prayer requests. A specific request is noticed when it's answered.

I was sharing the "ask for $100" request I shared previously in Chapter 4 in a discipling relationship when the man I was discipling said, "I had that happen to me today." I was a bit confused as the man I was discipling was a multimillionaire.

I asked for more information!

He said, "I was at a restaurant today, and my waitress used to work for me. I decided to leave a large cash tip on the table, but I only had several $100 dollar bills, so I left one of those."

When I left the restaurant and was walking to my car, the back door of the restaurant flew open, and the waitress ran out to me in the parking lot and gave me a huge hug. She said, "I just prayed this morning for $100 for a gas bill. Thank you. Your tip was an answer to my prayer."

Testimonies direct us from words on the pages of Scripture to an encounter with God, which then allows increased faith for ever-increasing specific requests.

The book of Revelation says:

> *The accuser of our brothers and sisters, the one who accuses them day and night before our God, has been thrown down. But they overcame him by the blood of the Lamb and by the word of their testimony, and they did not love their lives so much that they were afraid to die.* (Revelation 12:10b–12, NET)

The Apostle John writes that we overcome the accuser through testimony. Whether it's a testimony of an answered prayer or reading a verse of Scripture that gives needed wisdom for a decision—the more testimony, the better our discipleship.

Another testimony of answered prayer came on January 2, 1972, when I was staying at a Jesus House in Daytona Beach. Two of my friends came running into the house. Now, I'm a little rusty in Jesus Freak dialect, but I believe I remember most of the conversation.

> Two Jesus Freaks: "Wow, man, we ran out of gas in the VW bus."
>
> Me: "What happened?"
>
> Two Jesus Freaks: "Yeah, man, we prayed and asked God to put some gas in the tank."
>
> Me: "What happened?"
>
> Two Jesus Freaks: "Praise the Lord, man, the bus started again, and when we drove into the driveway, it stopped immediately."
>
> Me: "Far out, man!"

Testimonies, despite the dialect, are a necessary part of successful disciplemaking.

No Greater Feeling Than God Working Through Us

God has created us for a purpose. Yes, the God of the universe wants to use every believer in a unique way.

One evening, after sharing my testimony of how Jesus had changed my life, I asked if anyone would like to know Jesus as Lord and Savior. I think there were about forty in the room that night, and twenty raised their hands.

A pastor who had begun to mentor me said afterward, "There is no better feeling than God working through us to influence the life of another person."

I've never forgotten this statement, and I still experience that feeling every time that I disciple someone.

Only a relatively few believers can preach a sermon; a larger number can successfully lead a small group. But adding all the preachers, teachers, small group leaders, and worship leaders together in a local church still equals a minority of the members of that church who are experiencing God working through them in significant ministry.

With one-to-one discipleship, everyone can be a disciplemaker and have the Lord work through them.

I worked with a team training inmates in one-to-one discipleship at a correctional institution in Ohio. There were twenty-six in the first group we trained. We worked with these inmates for a few years in disciplemaking but were disconnected from them when the bureaucracy of the prison system shut us down.

One afternoon, we received a DVD created by the inmates. They had sent us a testimony video of their continued disciplemaking. After we left the prison, the inmates continued to disciple. They reported that hundreds had been discipled. And one of the prisoners summed up his thoughts on disciplemaking by saying:

There is no greater feeling than Jesus working through you to disciple another believer.

You Can Do This!

I learned in the early 1970s that if God can use Jesus Freaks to disciple, He can use you today, too. If God uses inmates in a correctional institution to disciple, He can use all of us!

I'm excited to share my journey in disciplemaking in this book.

But a word of caution—in the next chapter, I will discuss why everything I've written so far in this book might not work in your church.

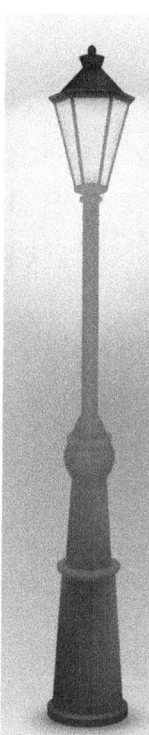

Review:

- LampPost Rule #1: Admit the problem.
- LampPost Rule #2: Know the right definition and content.
- LampPost Rule #3: Understand the blueprint.
- LampPost Rule #4: Know best practices.
- LampPost Rule #5: I can do this!

Has the lost art of Disciplemaking been rediscovered? Find out in *Interlude #5*.

Interlude #5:

The Lost Art of Disciplemaking

There isn't another command in Scripture more significant for the church than Jesus instructing us to *"go and make disciples"* (Matthew 28:19).

However, for many reasons, this command is ignored or implemented without the benefit of practical experience. Since the early centuries of Christianity, one-to-one disciplemaking has been lost.

Jesus said His authority and presence would be with us if we obeyed His commission. Obviously, something incredibly valuable is lost if we don't disciple.

When I first visited the St. Petersburg region of Russia in the early 1990s, I traveled to Pushkin for a tour of Catherine's Palace. Pushkin is also known as "the village of the Czars."

Walking through the palace, I entered a room that had nothing in it. There were no furniture, paintings, or elaborate wall hangings.

I thought it odd to have an empty room in a palace. With paying visitors, to make it interesting, shouldn't the administration at least drag a few treasures from storage and place them around the room?

Then, I noticed a cardboard display on an easel in the middle of the room. It included photos and written explanations of these photos in both Russian and English.

As I read, I realized this bare room was the fabled Amber Room.

The amber and other treasures from this room, once dubbed the "Eighth Wonder of the World," had been stolen by the Germans when they surrounded St. Petersburg during World War II.

The Amber Room, designed and built in Prussia, was gifted to Peter the Great and eventually installed in Catherine's Palace. That's why I was standing in an empty room. Anything placed in the room would seem inadequate or even desecrating.

The Amber Room once held six tons of amber in 335 differing hues, all designed into wall panels with intricate patterns. Added to the luxurious patina of amber in the room were thousands of gilded features—mirrors, gemstones, and statues of angels and children.

Everything was strategically highlighted with dozens of candelabras. The glimmering and glistening light on amber, mirrors, and golden statues created an unparalleled wonder.

In 2016, experts estimated the Amber Room's value at over $500 million. But as one curator said, "How can you really estimate the price of the *Eighth Wonder of the World*?"

But when World War II ended, the Russians discovered something of tremendous value and cultural worth was gone—stolen by the retreating German army. And it still hasn't been found.

In 1997, a few years after my vacant room experience with the Amber Room at Catherine's Palace, I entered another room. This one was at the Hermitage State Museum in downtown St. Petersburg, Russia.

I knew in advance this room wasn't empty, as my interpreter told me before we entered the room, "This room contains what we call *The Lost Art of World War II.*"

After the Russians pushed the Germans out of Russia and back to Germany, they returned the favor of the Germans stealing the Amber Room (and many thousands of other artworks) by taking thousands of paintings and other pieces of art from Germany.

For decades after World War II, the Russian government admitted nothing as to their involvement with this lost art. That is, they admitted nothing until the directors of the Hermitage sheepishly told the world in the mid-1990s that seventy-four of these lost paintings had been boxed in crates in the basement of the Hermitage.

Among the paintings crated in the basement were Degas's *Place de la Concorde;* one of Van Gogh's last paintings, *White House at Night;* and Renoir's sublime *In the Garden.*

And now these three paintings, along with dozens of others, were hung together—part of a display my interpreter said was titled *The Lost Art of World War II*!

Original Degas paintings have sold for over 50 million dollars, and only a few dozen people could afford a Renoir, as the last one went for $188 million at auction. No one can quite imagine how Van Gogh's *White House at Night,* with its "lost art" provenance, would be evaluated.

These paintings, all of them masterpieces, were lost—hammered into crates and stored in basement vaults, where they completely disappeared from view.

The same could be said about discipleship. It's hugely valuable . . . but in most churches it has disappeared from view.

Isn't it time we rediscovered the *Lost Art of Discipleship*?

Chapter 6:

The LampPost Strategy

Cheap grace is grace without discipleship.[13]

Years ago, a small church in Michigan invited me to hold a conference on discipleship.

I taught about one-to-one discipleship, the difference between foundational and formational discipleship, the four foundational disciplines, similar temptations, and best practices.

Basically, everything that you've read so far in this book.

It was a great conference. I felt inspired. Those attending listened and asked questions, and everyone committed to discipling one person per year for the rest of their lives. By the standards that I knew at the time, this conference couldn't have gone better.

After the conference, the pastor asked me to go to dinner with him and his wife. During our conversation, he asked, "Will the discipleship lessons that you just taught enable our church to start growing numerically?"

Too quickly, I said, "Of course!"

I was wrong.

From the Ashes of Defeat, I'm Praying for Victory!

I have many testimonies of success with one-to-one discipleship. I know *First Steps Conversations* works with new believers because I use it myself and have observed others discipling successfully.

It's been more difficult helping local churches to adopt one-to-one discipleship, though I've taught over one hundred discipling conferences in the United States and around the world.

The first five chapters of this book were about foundational discipleship. It works. You can do it! But will a local church pay the price organizationally to implement successful disciplemaking?

The next chapters of this book focus on implementing a workable one-to-one discipleship model in a local church or with a group of individuals from a variety of backgrounds who want to band together to focus on discipling their community.

I could list many organizations that I've talked to, consulted with, and held conferences at their locations, and they still have an 80 percent walk-away rate.

> **Successful one-to-one discipleship requires organizational change.**

Now, when asked if *First Steps Conversations* will work in a church or organization, I don't quickly answer, "Of course." Often, it doesn't work because successful one-to-one discipleship requires organizational change.

It's easy to say, "Wow!" while attending a conference and listening to new teaching. It's not easy to change the culture of disciplemaking inertia found in many churches and Christian organizations.

This chapter is entitled *The LampPost Strategy*. My aim in this chapter and the following chapters will be to discuss launching discipleship in a way that is workable and sustainable.

It takes sacrifice to develop a one-to-one disciplemaking culture. Local church vision could change, staffing will probably change, and buildings might not be needed.

Perhaps you should hide this book under a bushel and claim to others that you've never read it!

Sea of Galilee

> *Now the eleven disciples went to Galilee, to the mountain to which Jesus had directed them. And when they saw him they worshipped him, but some doubted. And Jesus came and said to them, "All authority in heaven and on earth has been given to me. Go therefore and make disciples of all nations."* (Matthew 28:16–19a, ESV)

I led a tour to Israel in the first week of March 2020.

Most tours spend a couple of nights on the shore of the Sea of Galilee. The hotel where we stayed was right on the bank of the sea. If you walked off the deck of the hotel, you would fall into the Sea of Galilee.

As mentioned throughout this book, the Great Commission has been the focal point of my ministry for forty-nine years. I founded a Jesus House in the early seventies that became a church, and I was the senior pastor of that church when I went to Israel.

At the hotel one morning, I got up to pray as I walked along the shoreline.

While praying, I felt God's Spirit moving within me. These words were given to me: *"Spend the rest of your time being faithful to the content that I have given to you."*

I knew what "content" meant, as my life message was the Great Commission.

What I found inspirational was that the Great Commission, given by Jesus to His disciples on the shore of the Sea of Galilee, was now being given to me as well—on the shore of the Sea of Galilee.

The LampPost Strategy

As I write this book, it's been a few years since my Sea of Galilee experience.

Arriving home from Israel in 2020, I finished a succession process in which a new senior pastor was hired to replace me at my former church. I was now able to fully focus on disciplemaking.

For years, I've watched individual believers, local churches, and Christian organizations agree about the need for discipleship. All would confirm that foundational discipleship was the best starting point.

Then, they would try to start a discipling ministry and fail.

What I've learned about sustainable discipleship is summed up in the phrase *The LampPost Strategy.*

That's LampPost Rule #6: Implement *The LampPost Strategy.*

This strategy has three components:

1. Content
2. Culture
3. Connections

The next chapters discuss content, how to build a disciple-producing culture, and developing the organizational support needed to connect disciplemakers with new or renewed followers who want to be discipled.

But first, a confession.

I'm not sure I know what I'm talking about.

I've learned by studying the Bible, reading other authors, and observing what works and doesn't work in overcoming "disciplemaking inertia" in organizations. Inertia is the tendency to do nothing or remain unchanged.

But I'm still learning!

Remember that few churches, denominations, or other Christian organizations are having success with disciplemaking. I want success, and I assume you're reading this book for the same reason. So let's agree to be in this together. Some of the ideas that I share will work, and some still need to be tested.

We can do this together!

Disciplemaking Inertia

> *For which of you, desiring to build a tower, does not first sit down and count the cost, whether he has enough to complete it? Otherwise, when he has laid a foundation and is not able to finish, all who see it begin to mock him.* (Luke 14:28–29, ESV)

If we agree Jesus is our Lord, then His last command to go and make disciples should be obeyed. But most believers don't disciple or even know how to disciple.

But something even more insidious is afoot: even those with a passion for discipleship don't often disciple.

Recently, I sat down with a former editor at one of the most successful publishing organizations in the USA. We were discussing discipleship, and he said, "There are about 1,200 books about discipleship on Kindle. Do you know how many searches there were on Kindle last month for discipleship books?"

Having recently attended conferences on discipleship that were at capacity, I responded, "I would think about 20,000 searches for discipleship books last month."

He smiled and said, "No, about 550."

When it comes to discipleship, the church is often far more willing to talk about it than do it.

Like I said, disciplemaking inertia.

As one conference speaker I heard recently said, "All the problems of the world today have one cause—the failure of the church to disciple."

There are three reasons that the church doesn't disciple or that, when they do, it's not effective.

First: Content

Any believer can disciple, but correct content is a key to success.

If the proper foundation of content isn't laid, the building won't be built, and 80 percent of those who proclaim Jesus will walk away from faithfulness.

The content of foundational discipleship must be laser-focused on the needs of a new follower's first three months. Let's review good content and best practices:

- Foundational disciplines
- Similar temptations
- One-to-one
- First three months' emphasis

Though foundational content is rigid, it allows the development of an individual calling and the formational discipleship needed to walk faithfully in that calling.

- Foundational discipleship is the same for all believers, and formational discipleship is different for all believers.
- Foundational discipleship is one-to-one, while formational discipleship can have mentors, professors, teachers, and coaches, as needed, for a follower's individual calling.

To overcome disciplemaking inertia, the church must understand the difference between foundational and formational discipleship. Since formational discipleship has been the unsuccessful norm for discipling new believers in many churches, having a paradigm shift to an understanding of foundational discipleship is imperative.

> *Having a paradigm shift to an understanding of foundational discipleship is imperative.*

I recently spoke on foundational discipleship at a small church.

The church pastor and other leaders listened carefully to my teaching about foundational and formational discipleship, then I stopped and asked if there were questions:

First question: How does your teaching that 80 percent of new believers walk away from faithfulness square with eternal security?

Second question: Can't we just take your book and use it in a small group?

Third question: Do you think discipleship is a man's thing and not just a woman's thing?

Fourth question: What are your analytics of success, and how can we know that we will be successful if we follow your plan?

My initial thought about these questions was, "This church is more concerned about the jot and tittle of traditions and analytic success than discipleship." But I was more circumspect in my response because I knew their questions came from not just a lack of knowledge but from their culture of disciplemaking inertia.

Which brings me to:

Second: Culture

None of us will disciple without encouragement.
The book of Hebrews says:

> *Not neglecting to meet together, as is the habit of some, but encouraging one another, and all the more as you see the Day drawing near.* (Hebrews 10:25, ESV)

There isn't a lot of encouragement for disciplemaking in churches, as most Christians don't disciple.

To overcome disciplemaking inertia in a local church or community, there must be testimonies of encouragement. *The LampPost Strategy* develops a team that shines the light of disciplemaking into a church or community.

The culture of disciplemaking isn't an individual pursuit. Culture, at its core, is a group effort. For discipleship to grow and maintain effectiveness, a group of disciplers must believe and work together with four guiding lights.

> First, a commitment to the Great Commission in Matthew 28 and a willingness to make it a primary objective in all aspects of church organization.

> Second, an understanding of the need for "one another" testimonies of support and encouragement.

> Third, an emphasis on the formational calling of all believers that can only be developed and sustained through foundational discipleship.

> Fourth, a willingness both to pay the price in resourcing the Great Commission with time, talents, and finances and to joyfully employ discipleship practices that blast through discipleship inertia.

I've always kept notes of encouraging comments given to me. I guess it could be pride, but it is also much needed, as promoting discipleship can be frustrating.

I recently added the following note from a friend (a very successful writer). It was a compliment to me and my team in our efforts at First Steps Discipleship (GrantEdwardsAuthor.com).

> *I was reminded yesterday of why I appreciate your quest to make discipleship more than a good intention.*

> *Not so long ago, I had a meeting with an editor who wanted my help with a project. I asked for more details and was dismayed to hear that, while it was reassuring to readers, it was far from biblically accurate.*

It championed Jesus' love, which is fine. It called people to get to know Jesus. Also a good thing. It spoke of how he's coming back for us to gather us into an eternity with him.

And then it . . . stopped.

No need for obedience was mentioned. No shouldering a cross and no narrow path.

This wasn't a product about Jesus. It was a product about squishy Jesus. A Jesus with no spine, no claim on the lives of his followers, a cuddly night-light version of Jesus.

When I asked what happened to discipleship, I was met with a blank stare. It was there, I was told. No, it isn't, I said. And then I heard what convinced me to walk away fast:

"Times are hard. This is what people need to hear these days."

No, it isn't. Because it isn't true. It certainly isn't complete. Jesus is coming back as a judge, riding a warhorse, and with legions of angels behind him.

Cuddly?

We'll all hit the deck not just because we respect the idea of Jesus but because that's what you do when a tornado roars directly at you. Even if you're confident you're safe, you cringe before the sheer power and majesty of something or someone whose power is so immense.

You're preparing people to be safe at Discipling Another . . . now and forever . . . to live lives of purpose and power . . . now and forever.

No squishiness in the discipleship that you preach, Grant.

Thanks. You're needed.

This email from my friend arrived during the middle of a week when I was experiencing constant frustration in my efforts to encourage disciplemaking around the world.

Culture either works for discipleship or against it. We all need a LampPost culture of encouragement!

Third: Connections

In a later chapter, I will discuss the tenets of building proper connections and organization for keeping momentum in discipleship.

Here is the simple rule: the law of supply and demand.

If you have someone who wants to disciple and doesn't have a person to disciple, there will be frustration. And on the opposite end of the equation is the frustration of having people needing to be discipled with no disciplers available.

At the beginning of this chapter, I told the story of the pastor who asked if the discipleship material that I had just shared with his congregation would enable his church to finally grow. And as I confessed, I quickly said, "Yes."

I had good reason, as over one hundred people from his church stood at the end of the conference and committed to discipling one person per year for the rest of their lives.

How can a church not grow with this type of response and enthusiasm?

Well, they won't grow if there's no one to disciple!

The supply and demand of disciplers and disciples must equal each other.

If a church has 100 needing to be discipled, that church must also have 100 disciplers. A church's capacity for effective evangelism is equal to the number of disciplers in that church. Evangelism without disciplers loses 80 percent.

I have a pastor who sent me a note explaining that over four hundred Ukrainians had accepted Jesus in Düsseldorf, Germany, recently—his problem was that he had no one to disciple them.

Consider this law of supply and demand with disciplers and disciples. If there are disciplers with no one to disciple, that's a problem. If there are those wanting to be discipled, and no disciplers, that's a problem too.

Both disciplers and disciples must be equal in numbers to eliminate disciplemaking inertia.

In a later chapter, I will discuss how to equalize disciplers with disciples in a discussion of 3rd generation disciplers—but be patient as there are still several chapters to be read before we solve the problem of supply and demand in discipleship.

Review:
- LampPost Rule #1: Admit the problem.
- LampPost Rule #2: Know the right definition and content.
- LampPost Rule #3: Understand the blueprint.
- LampPost Rule #4: Know best practices.
- LampPost Rule #5: I can do this!
- LampPost Rule #6: Implement *The LampPost Strategy*.

Thank you for reading this far in this book. Check the strength of your foundational disciplines by taking "The Test" in *Interlude #6*.

Interlude #6:

The Test

Below are my favorite verses of Scripture that support the four foundational disciplines of the Christian faith.

The Bible:

> *Therefore put away all filthiness and rampant wickedness and receive with meekness the implanted word, which is able to save your souls.* (James 1:21, ESV)

Prayer:

> *Do not be anxious about anything, but in everything by prayer and supplication with thanksgiving let your requests be made known to God.* (Philippians 4:6)

Fellowship:

> *Not neglecting to meet together, as is the habit of some, but encouraging one another, and all the more as you see the Day drawing near.* (Hebrews 10:25)

Discipling:

> *And what you have heard from me in the presence of many witnesses entrust to faithful men, who will be able to teach others also.* (2 Timothy 2:2)

Our disciplines should be assessed regularly to make sure that the foundation is stable and secure. Our spiritual formation and calling will only withstand storms if we have a solid foundation.

When I discuss a significant spiritual struggle with another follower of Jesus, I often ask the following four questions to assess the strength of their foundation with Jesus.

Let's go ahead and take the test ourselves:

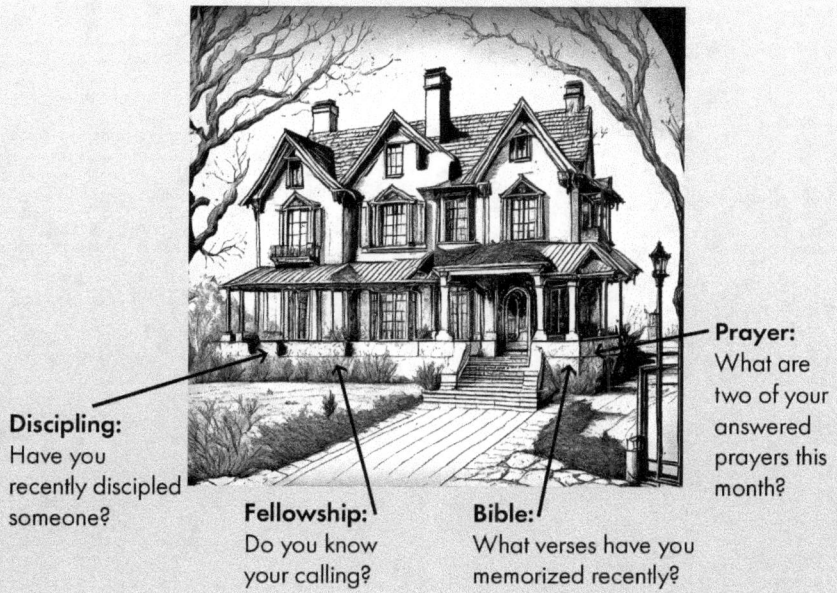

Discipling: Have you recently discipled someone?

Fellowship: Do you know your calling?

Bible: What verses have you memorized recently?

Prayer: What are two of your answered prayers this month?

How did you do?

I hope that you said "yes" four times.

If we are not memorizing Scripture, have no recently answered prayers, don't know our calling, and have never discipled someone—our foundation needs to be repaired. Our faith will not support our growth in Christ without the right foundational disciplines.

As our foundational disciplines mature, the motive behind the disciplines grows from our determination to love. Loving Jesus must be the sustaining motive for the four foundational disciplines.

Chapter 7:

Content ~ Same for the Foundation, Different for the Formation

Therefore, brothers, be all the more diligent to confirm your calling and election, for if you practice these qualities you will never fall. (2 Peter 1:10, ESV)

Calling is the purpose of our lives.

Every follower of Jesus has a unique purpose designed and monitored by God through spiritual gifts and ministry opportunities. It's an individual and narrow path.

Our calling should dictate our career, job, and education. Living according to calling means everything swirls around your purpose in life, as Os Guinness writes in his book *The Call*:

> *What do I mean by "calling"? For the moment let me say simply that calling is the truth that God calls us to himself so decisively that everything we are, everything we do, and everything we have is invested with a special devotion and dynamism lived out as a response to his summons and service.*[14]

When we find our calling, we find purpose with everything in our lives coming into alignment. There is no greater joy than doing what God created us for.

Through calling, we live in the pocket of God's will.

I've heard people say, "I'm happy; I believe that I was made to do this." I've also heard many say, "I hate to get up in the morning. I have another fifteen years before I can retire."

I've spent decades working within my calling. I didn't find my calling through personality tests or gift assessments. Rather, God led me, as a young believer, into disciplemaking.

That's my calling. What is your calling?

Foundation to Calling to Formation

Here's a formula to find and live in your calling: foundational discipling results in believers finding their calling, and formational discipling then enables those believers to live out that calling.

Foundation to Calling to Formation!

The content of foundational discipleship is the same for all followers, and the content of formational discipleship is different for all believers.

I am a pastor, and a friend of mine is a medical doctor. We have the same four foundational disciplines, but our callings have dictated our formational disciplines. I went to seminary and my friend graduated from medical school.

Contact me if you want to know the historical background of the Gospel of Matthew. However, if you need surgery, you should see my friend! I can do a great job dissecting Scripture but not removing your gallbladder.

All believers have the same foundation, but we have different callings. Calling is built upon a solid foundation, and we'll be fulfilled in our occupation if it aligns with our calling.

Let's remember *Foundation to Calling to Formation* with the same content for the foundation but differing content for the formation.

Chapter 7: Content ~ Same for the Foundation, Different for the Formation

Always Being Built

I've traveled to St. Petersburg, Russia, over sixty times.

On many of those trips, I visited a small city outside of St. Petersburg named Kommunar.

Early in the 1990s, the team that I worked with planted a church in Kommunar. The name of the city translated into English means "communist man," so it seemed a great place to start a church!

The road to Kommunar passes through Pushkin, which is known as the Czars' Village.

Why?

As we drive through Pushkin, we pass the Alexander Palace, where the last czar lived with his family until they were arrested by the communists. Keep driving, and we pass Catherine's Palace, a marvelous blue palace that now contains a replica of the fabled Amber Room.

But that's not all the palaces.

Keep going a few more kilometers, and we enter another small village named Pavlovsk. What do we find in this village? Yes, another palace, built for Paul—Catherine the Great's son.

That's the Czars' Village and the surrounding area—palace after palace after palace. And on the road to Kommunar, after the three palaces, we might expect to find another palace. Instead, we pass a large foundation. Palace after palace after palace and then a large cement foundation.

I'm a pastor and writer who uses the image of a "foundation" in my sermons, speaking engagements, and writing, so I took an interest in this foundation. After a few years, I noticed that no buildings were built on the foundation and that the foundation kept getting larger.

I can get obsessed with details that no one else notices or cares about, and I admit as the years passed, I was more interested in driving by that foundation than the palaces.

Would there be a new palace, a factory, or an apartment building of Russian flats?

On my last drive-by of the foundation, it extended along the road for about a kilometer, but it still had nothing on it. I mentioned the ever-increasing and nothing-built-on foundation to my interpreter, and he said, "We have a phrase in Russia which means 'always being built.'"

A Strategy for Disciplemaking and Spiritual Formation

It's odd to have a foundation without a structure.

My interpreter went on to explain that the "always being built" foundation on the road to Kommunar resulted from differing mayors in that region taking over the project from the previous mayor and either stopping, restarting, or changing the project altogether.

With no clear plan, vision, or calling, the foundation was always being built.

A foundation undergirds an architect's design for a building. A foundation shouldn't just "sit in a pew" (oops!) year after year outside of a small village in Russia without a building on it.

Some believers stop their foundation-to-calling-to-formation process and they get stuck in place. There's no growth, no serving, no building on a solid foundation. And sadly, they may not even know there's more they could be experiencing.

> **It's impossible to move from foundation to formation without a calling or direction.**

It's impossible to move from foundation to formation without a calling or direction.

Jesus is the Cornerstone, Paul laid the foundation, and now we build!

The content of our foundation is the same for everyone, but because of calling, our formational content is different.

Paul writes:

> *According to the grace of God given to me, like a skilled master builder I laid a foundation, and someone else is building upon it. Let each one take care how he builds upon it. For no one can lay*

> *a foundation other than that which is laid, which is Jesus Christ.* (1 Corinthians 3:10–11, ESV)

The Cornerstone and the foundation are fixed.

Jesus can't be changed. Okay, I'm going out on an exegetical limb here, but the summation of Pauline thought in his epistles easily leads to the four foundational disciplines of the faith being Bible, prayer, fellowship, and evangelism/discipleship. Now, one scooch further out on my exegetical limb and we discover Jesus is the unchangeable Cornerstone. Paul's foundation still exists for all disciples today and our personal calling, or formation, builds upon this foundation.

This is the strategy for both disciplemaking and spiritual formation. Jesus is the Cornerstone. Paul (and the rest of Scripture) teaches a foundation that's the same today for all believers, but we need to know our calling to build our ministry.

As Paul says:

> *Now, if anyone builds on the foundation with gold, silver, precious stones, wood, hay, straw—each one's work will become manifest, for the Day will disclose it, because it will be revealed by fire, and the fire will test what sort of work each one has done. If the work that anyone has built on the foundation survives, he will receive a reward. If anyone's work is burned up, he will suffer loss, though he himself will be saved, but only as through fire.* (1 Corinthians 3:12–15, ESV)

Foundation to calling to formation yields ministry and service that will survive the fire of even latter-day tribulation.

It's a house built on the Rock! It's gold, not straw.

That's LampPost Rule #7: Foundation to Calling to Formation

From Jesus to Calling to Russia

In 1994, I invited a businessman from a major food distribution company to travel to Russia with me. His family owned this business, and with him leading the sales department, sales had grown from about twenty million to over one hundred million dollars a year.

Yet, he felt that he wasn't fulfilling God's will in his life.

In the early 1990s, there was a major revival in the area surrounding St. Petersburg, Russia, and I wanted him to see what God was doing there.

Visiting Russia wasn't easy. Food was in short supply and lodging was atrocious. Communist Russia had within itself the seeds of its own destruction.

As revival often proves, when a land or culture is faithless, God is even more faithful, and hundreds of thousands of Russians were becoming followers of Jesus. Even though the necessities of life were in short supply, God's grace was abundant.

My friend had developed an interest in cell groups (or small groups) at his local church in Cincinnati, Ohio. He was reading a book on cell groups written by Ralph Neighbour while traveling around St. Petersburg watching thousands accept Jesus as Lord and Savior.

On the plane back to the USA, my friend told me that he wanted to bring cell-based teaching to Russia. My response was more incredulous than serious as I thought, *Yeah, a businessman with two weeks of short-term mission experience wants to teach the churches of Russia about cell groups.*

As we talked, he explained, "The churches in Russia need to learn about cell groups. I think I can get Ralph Neighbour's books translated into Russian and printed in Russia, and then I want to travel the country teaching churches about cell-based churches."

My response to my friend was, "Russia is huge. It has eleven time zones. When we left the Cincinnati airport to travel to St. Petersburg, Russia, the entire distance from Cincinnati to St. Petersburg is the same distance from St. Petersburg on the western edge of Russia to Vladivostok on the eastern edge of Russia."

And I asked, "How are you going to teach this entire nation about small groups? It will cost hundreds of thousands of dollars!"

And yet, that is what my friend did. All of it.

After translating Ralph Neighbour's books into Russian and starting a publishing house in Russia to print the books, he traveled the entire country over four years, teaching hundreds of churches about cell groups.

Today, if you travel to Russia (not easy with current events), most of the pastors of large churches have cell groups, and those groups began after the pastor attended a conference led by my friend.

Why do I share this story?

I discipled my friend—foundational discipleship—and he learned to hear God's voice. God told him to change his business card from "business leader" to "missionary."

He obeyed his calling at tremendous cost (yes, it did cost him hundreds of thousands of dollars), but he influenced a country. With the current persecution of churches in Russia, his ministry of transforming traditional churches to cell-based congregations still has a tremendous impact.

Foundation, to calling, to formation, to changing a nation!

Calling Revisited

We read in the book of Ephesians:

> *I therefore, a prisoner for the Lord, urge you to walk in a manner worthy of the calling to which you have been called.* (Ephesians 4:1, ESV)

Look at your fingertips. They are one of a kind. No one else has your fingerprints.

Consider your calling. It is one of a kind. No other person has your calling!

The uniqueness of your calling is why Paul encourages you to walk in a manner worthy of this calling. The Greek word for "worthy" is "axis." Often, when we read Scripture in English, nuance is lost in the translation.

An axis is an imaginary line about which a body rotates. Our calling is like the sun rotating on its axis or the earth on its axis. It should dictate our career, job, education, money, and those with whom we associate.

Calling is the focal point. But there is an "if/then" with calling.

If God has given us a calling, then He has also given us spiritual gifts for that calling. If God has given us a calling, then prayers asked according to calling will be answered. If God has given us a calling, then our peace and happiness will be experienced by focusing on our calling.

Do you know your calling? Many don't, wandering from job to differing careers with frustrated relationships, often aimless in life and easily discouraged.

Finding our calling aligns our faith with God's will. There is no greater peace. Let's continue growing from foundation to calling to formation to having a fulfilled life of serving Jesus.

Calling and Relationship with Jesus

I wrote this book with a goal expressed below:

> *To this end we always pray for you, that our God may make you worthy of his calling and may fulfill every resolve for good and every work of faith by his power,* (2 Thessalonians 1:11, ESV)

Christianity is not a religion; it is a relationship with God, and discipleship must focus on this relationship.

A great relationship has communication. God talks to us, and we talk to God—it isn't God just talking while we listen or us talking, hoping God is listening. As we walk with Jesus, a growing sense of His presence allows us to converse intimately.

Not too long ago, I read the following:

We need to understand that being with Jesus is the ultimate pursuit of our lives. Being with Jesus always comes before doing anything. Doing flows from being, not the other way around. This is a crucial principle for anyone who wants to live as a faithful follower of Jesus: the primary call on my life is not to do something for Jesus; the primary call on my life is to be with Jesus.[15]

The content of discipleship—both foundational and formational—must have the goal of a conversant relationship with Jesus in which His calling is revealed. When we obey His calling, we build with gold and silver.

> *For all who are led by the Spirit of God are children of God.* (Romans 8:14, NLT)

Let's remember:

- Calling comes from a relationship with Jesus.
- Foundational content is the same for all believers, while formational content will be different.
- As we follow Jesus, the foundation stays the same, but our calling can change, and with it, our formational disciplines will change.

Content/Culture/Connections

To develop sustainable discipleship, for your LampPost to stay lit, a church or group of followers interested in encouraging one-to-one discipleship must have the right content, culture, and connections.

> "Followers interested in encouraging one-to-one discipleship must have the right content, culture, and connections."

All three must be developed together. In the next chapter, we'll discuss the culture of disciplemaking.

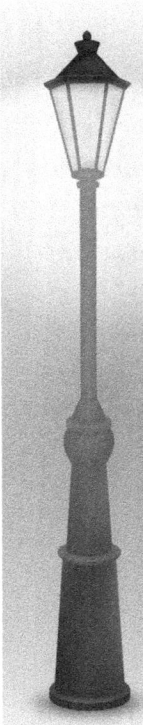

Review:
- LampPost Rule #1: Admit the problem.
- LampPost Rule #2: Know the right definition and content.
- LampPost Rule #3: Understand the blueprint.
- LampPost Rule #4: Know best practices.
- LampPost Rule #5: I can do this!
- LampPost Rule #6: Implement *The LampPost Strategy*.
- LampPost Rule #7: Foundation to Calling to Formation.

Both newborn babies and newborn believers have similar developmental needs. *Interlude #7* is a provocative look at children without parents.

Interlude #7:

Orphans

Religion that is pure and undefiled before God the Father is this: to visit orphans and widows in their affliction, and to keep oneself unstained from the world. (James 1:27, ESV)

My wife traveled to Romania in 1991 with a group from our church that had listened to a newscast on ABC's 20/20 entitled *Shame of a Nation* describing thousands of orphans in Romania. They were held in "child gulags" created by the dictator Nicolae Ceaușescu.

Parents couldn't afford to keep the babies at home and abandoned them on the doorsteps of the orphanages.

The orphanages had few workers and the babies were left by themselves in cribs with little human interaction except for feeding and changing diapers. If you entered these orphanages, you would think there would be the screams and crying of unattended babies.

The exact opposite happened in the orphanages. The rooms holding the babies were strangely silent.

No crying or screams—just bumping, bumping, and bumping. The infants had stopped crying when no one responded to their cries and were now rocking themselves silently in their cribs.

The simultaneous sound of cribs bumping into one another filled the orphanage.

Psychologists have since concluded that many of these orphans developed attachment disorders, creating difficulties in forming meaningful relationships later in life.

A psychologist writing in an article in *The Atlantic* magazine said that when he first began studying these orphans, he didn't realize that seeking comfort for distress from another human was a learned behavior with all babies. He said in the article:

Those children had no idea that an adult could make them feel better. Imagine how that must feel—to be miserable and not even know that another human being could help.[16]

Has this happened with first-time followers of Jesus in the church today?

Newborn babies can have developmental needs without a one-to-one relationship; how about born-again believers today? As with infants, do we understand that seeking comfort from other believers, walking in unity, and having a conversant relationship with Jesus are learned behaviors?

A healthy attachment between a mom and child is needed to develop love, the ability to communicate, and emotional health.

We must understand that the qualities of spiritual formation are best learned in a one-to-one discipling relationship. Are we raising generations of believers who, because of a lack of disciplemaking, haven't learned to speak the truth in love, value meaningful connections in fellowship, and lack spiritual maturity?

Our churches shouldn't be filled with the silent bumping of inadequacy but life and joy in the Spirit.

Chapter 8:

A Culture of Sustainable Disciplemaking

What you have learned and received and heard and seen in me—practice these things, and the God of peace will be with you. (Philippians 4:9, ESV)

There's a litmus test for telling if a church has a culture of sustainable discipleship, and it's this frequently heard question:

"Have you been discipled?"

That's the question asked by those who've been discipled once they recognize they need to also be disciplemakers.

Believers who ask that question have discovered that disciplemaking is more than just *being* discipled. They know they need to *disciple others* too. And they've experienced the joy of God working through them to impact the lives of others.

Does a visitor or new member of your church hear that question? Not if your church is like most churches today.

Disciplemaking as a culture has been lost.

Repositioning

I'm often asked, "How is retirement?"

After forty-nine years of being the senior pastor at one church in the same community and then leaving this church, I sense the concern and friendliness lying behind the question. But I also don't like the question because I'm spiritually allergic to the concept of retirement.

My response is, "I didn't retire; I repositioned myself."

Usually, that's enough of an answer to get the conversation back to the topic of the cold, gray, rainy Ohio weather. But a few insist on a more detailed explanation by asking a follow-up question: "And what does 'repositioning' mean?"

My answer is always the same: "I'm working with followers of Jesus, local churches, and mission organizations to develop a culture of sustainable discipleship."

Unfortunately, that comment tends to silence further conversation.

But since you're still reading, I'm thinking you care about discipleship. And you're even eager for a deeper explanation of the "culture of sustainable discipleship."

So here we go.

From Senior Pastor to Disciplemaking

One of the frustrations during my last ten years as a senior pastor was my lack of time to understand and develop sustainable discipleship. Our church was discipling, but only a percentage of those who had been discipled were disciplemaking.

I wanted to find a way to challenge those who'd been discipled to make a commitment to disciple at least one person a year for the rest of their lives. I wanted to see us embrace a culture of disciplemaking that led to sustainable discipleship.

To do this, I needed to step away as the organizational leader of a local church. Why? Because much of what I was doing as a pastor hindered my calling to disciple disciples who disciple.

Chapter 8: A Culture of Sustainable Disciplemaking

I've heard the following quote attributed to C. S. Lewis, one of my favorite authors. I don't know if he actually said it, but if he didn't, he should have.

> *There exists in every church something that sooner or later works against the very purpose for which it came into existence. So, we must strive very hard, by the grace of God, to keep the church focused on the mission that Christ originally gave to it.*

Jesus was clear about the mission of the church. Let's check His Great Commission again:

> *And Jesus came and said to them, "All authority in heaven and on earth has been given to me. Go therefore and make disciples of all nations, baptizing them in the name of the Father and of the Son and of the Holy Spirit, teaching them to observe all that I have commanded you. And behold, I am with you always, to the end of the age." (Matthew 28:18–20, ESV)*

And there it is—disciplemaking. *Sustainable* discipleship.

Don't get me wrong, I loved being the pastor of a church.

But preaching, sitting on committees, fundraising, and attending to other administrative aspects of a church, while necessary, aren't one-to-one discipleship. They aren't dead-center focused on what Jesus asks any church to be about. There's nothing wrong with planning and being organized, but I began asking myself a question, which was a paraphrase of the quote above.

> *The purpose of the church is the Great Commission. Is my role as senior pastor allowing me to fulfill the purpose in the ministry to which I'm called? Am I developing sustainable one-to-one discipleship?*

Since my retirement (oops, repositioning), I've been available full-time to help churches, mission organizations, and individuals in local communities develop sustainable one-to-one discipleship. I get to do this full-time, but if you're a pastor or church leader still serving in a pastoral role, know this: you can do it without having to retire.

It's needed. It's purposeful. And best of all, it's possible.

Let's Revisit the Three C's of Discipleship

For discipleship to be sustainable, there must be content, culture, and connections.

Many discipleship programs, methods, and books don't work because they either have the wrong content, fail to address creating a disciplemaking culture, or simply can't connect disciplers with disciples.

And some discipling efforts fail on all three fronts.

I was interviewed by a major publisher a few years ago.

Aware of the growing need for discipleship, they wanted to create and promote discipling material. I discussed with them the difference between foundational and formational discipleship—along with the importance of one-to-one discipling in the first ninety days.

We had a nice conversation.

I could tell they didn't understand the difference between foundational and formational discipling. This publisher had for years experienced great success creating Christian educational books and curriculum—all of it good stuff. But I suspected few on their team had ever discipled a new believer.

They thanked me for my time and then developed and printed their discipleship materials. The program was written by a team of talented writers with input from other pastors, Bible teachers, and scholars. The material was printed on glossy paper, interactive in small-group settings, and laid out with top-notch design and illustrations.

At a cost of roughly a million dollars.

I recently asked about the success of this material and was told, "It's pretty much all still sitting in a warehouse. They didn't sell much of it. And I think the few churches that used it didn't get much out of it."

While the program was well-intentioned, it didn't deliver discipleship because it didn't address content, culture, and connections.

And those are the three C's essential for sustainable discipleship: content, culture, and connections. All three must be understood and included for disciplemaking to be sustainable.

- Content: Foundational/Calling/Formational, which has already been discussed, but I will share best practices in Chapters 11 and 12.
- Culture: Nothing of significance can happen without the right culture. I discuss culture in this chapter.
- Connections: There's an organizational aspect of discipleship, along with analytics, to guide success. I will discuss connections in Chapter 9.

Without addressing content, culture, and connections, efforts at sustained disciplemaking will inevitably fail.

What is Culture?

Peter Drucker, perhaps the most influential business consultant of the last one hundred years, is often quoted as saying, "Culture eats strategy for breakfast."[17]

I've seen this statement by Drucker mentioned in most books I've read about culture. And since "culture" has such an appetite for consuming our plans, strategies, intentions, and goals, I thought understanding it could help me tame this ravenous beast that eats strategies and plans.

> *Without addressing content, culture, and connections, efforts at sustained disciplemaking will inevitably fail.*

Thousands of books and articles have been written about culture . . . but what is it? I searched but couldn't find a simple definition. For many, defining "culture" has been as elusive as finding Sasquatch. In our search, we believe we've found it and know what it is, but then "culture" disappears back into a mountainous wood before being captured and understood.

And, like Bigfoot, all sorts of people report sightings. They're there in books, TV documentaries, and tucked into YouTube streaming channels. Yet even with all the media hubbub and breathless proclamations of new insights, an actual Yeti has yet to be found.

Certainly, defining culture would be easier than finding Bigfoot. I tried, I really did, but found only frustration.

Then, I read an article in *Harvard Business Review* chronicling a research project on culture. Imagine my surprise when the experts concluded what I had discovered in my study of culture—that a generally accepted definition of culture doesn't exist.

Take *that*, Sasquatch!

The article said, "Numerous processes exist for creating [culture] and changing it. Agreement on specifics [of culture] is sparse across these definitions, models, and methods."[18]

There you have it. I'm not crazy. My frustrations were legitimized by *HBR*!

But I was left with the same question: How can we satiate Peter Drucker's culture beast if we can't define it?

Fortunately, the same article reported that after examining hundreds if not thousands of descriptions of culture, four distinct points seemed to be essential components in any usable definition of culture.

We might not have a firm definition, but we could at least know how the beast looks, feels, walks, and smells.

Those four components are:

Shared: Culture is a group phenomenon. It can't exist solely with a single person.

Pervasive: Culture permeates multiple levels and applies broadly in an organization. It manifests in behaviors, rituals, symbols, stories, and legends.

Enduring: Culture can direct the thoughts and actions of group members over the long term.

Implicit: Culture has a subliminal nature, and people are effectively hardwired to recognize and respond to it instinctively. It acts as a kind of silent language.

I was delighted to see that the best practices of the business world are already found in the Bible. Jesus' Great Commission can be shared and is pervasive, enduring, and implicit. The command of Jesus "to go and make disciples" should be the culture of the church.

We may not have an all-encompassing Biblical definition of church culture, but we know how it looks and feels when members of a church constantly ask:

"Have you been discipled?"

That's LampPost Rule #8: Have you been discipled?

A Culture of Sustainable Discipleship

If the culture of a church supports discipleship, then disciplemaking is shared, becomes pervasive in branding and messaging, endures through good and bad times, and implicitly underlies activities and conversations within a church.

A church with sustainable discipleship sets goals, builds programs, and hires staff to support disciplemaking. Let's consider how sustainable discipleship is shared, pervasive, enduring, and implicit.

Disciplemaking Is Shared

"Shared" implies similar values, actions, and attitudes. A shared culture has unwritten rules and assumptions of behavior. Sustained disciplemaking happens when a church decides that discipleship will become its story.

Churches and individual believers have differing attitudes and societal expressions. There are differing races, languages, and customs, but they are all on the receiving end of Jesus' last command: go and make disciples.

Discipleship is the foundational calling shared by all believers. Yes, there are differing formational callings for every believer, but foundational discipleship is shared by everyone who loves Jesus as their Lord and Savior.

Individual believers are given spiritual gifts along with unique personality traits and abilities. Some teach while others can hit three-pointers on the basketball court. Jesus gives differing gifts to His followers but only one Commission—to go and make disciples.

(Read Chapter 3 again for a discussion on the difference between foundational and formational discipleship.)

When teaching discipleship, I use the phrase, "You can do this!" because Jesus doesn't ask you to do something that you and He together can't do.

Not everyone can preach, lead worship, or write like C. S. Lewis or Timothy Keller, but all believers can disciple.

We can do this!

Sustained Discipleship Is Pervasive

Successful disciplemaking is driven by excited disciplers sharing testimonies about God working through them. There's authority abiding in discipleship. Jesus said, *"All authority has been given to me; therefore, go and make disciples."*

Have you ever noticed the confidence and joy of a person walking in authority? You can see and hear it. They're comfortable in their own skin; they aren't thrown by the unexpected.

Believers don't need to be famous, wealthy, or influential to walk in authority—they just need to be obedient.

My wife and I vacation regularly in Charleston, South Carolina, and we often stay at a Marriott® in the downtown area.

Chapter 8: A Culture of Sustainable Disciplemaking

My basic requirement for a hotel is that I can get some sleep. I have status at the Marriott chain, which means I often get a room on a high floor, away from the elevator and ice machine, and that room is sometimes upgraded to an even better room.

But I don't go to a Marriott hotel for a better room. I go because at Marriott hotels, I find a comfortable bed and a quiet environment, and I'm able to sleep.

But that didn't happen one night. Not at all. I got exactly no sleep.

It started with a crowd of noisy college students walking down the hallway and continued when they partied in the room next to ours until 3 a.m. On cue, the air conditioning unit launched into a death rattle, banging, and gasping for an hour until it stopped altogether.

At 4 a.m.

I know because I was watching the clock instead of sleeping. I also know the temperature in the room increased quickly from my optimal sleeping temperature of 69 degrees to 92 degrees because I got out of bed to check the thermostat.

From 5 to 6 a.m., I prayed—and not selfless prayers of history-changing power. Mostly, I prayed to patiently endure my Marriott trials like Job in the Bible—to calm down, to relax, to be able to sleep.

At 6 a.m., I gave up and went downstairs to get breakfast.

As I walked into the dining room, a young man was cleaning a table. He asked me, "How was your night here at the Marriott?"

While reading this book, you've learned that I'm a Christian, and as a Christian, I refrain from cursing even in desperate circumstances.

But I did tell this young man all my problems from the night before. I was frustrated, so it took a few minutes. The young man listened carefully, nodding his head in sympathy, and then said something unexpected.

"That was a rough night. Let me buy you breakfast, and when your wife comes down, I'll buy her breakfast too."

I accepted the free breakfast. But later that day, feeling guilty about taking the young man's money, I went to the manager, offering to pay for the two breakfasts.

The manager said that the breakfasts didn't cost the young man anything. That all the employees at this Marriott had the authority to offer a free breakfast to anyone complaining about a bad night.

What an empowering slice of authority, and every Marriott employee at that hotel had it. Here's the truth: every member of a church, both staff and members, also has the authority (and command) to ask the question, "Have you been discipled?"

So why don't we hear the question more often?

Disciplemaking Is Enduring

Endurance indicates a long-haul mentality. Culture should be lasting, not easily dismissed or derailed by distractions, interruptions, or competing values.

The Great Commission to make disciples should be the most enduring and practical vision, mission, and purpose of a local church. This doesn't negate the importance of worship, preaching, or other ministries like food pantries, but it gives the foundation for the success of everything a church does.

Unfortunately, disciplemaking has not been the enduring culture of churches today.

I wrote previously that only 5 percent of churches in the USA have a reproducing disciplemaking culture. Most churches do help disciples grow, but the picture painted by the Great Commission isn't a disciple sitting in a pew but rather a disciple doing disciplemaking wherever the disciple goes.[19]

One-to-one disciplemaking provides a depth of spiritual development not found in worship services or even small groups. Despite the hundreds of thousands of church sanctuaries in the USA and countless small groups, enduring faith is in short supply. Let's consider the following chain of statistics about disciplemaking.

Starting with one hundred new believers, all having just accepted Jesus in a church service one morning.

- 80 percent of these new followers will walk away from faithfulness soon after their decision to follow Jesus.

That leaves twenty.

- Of those twenty, only about 20 percent will continue growing dynamically in Christ.[20]

That leaves four.

Take the four left from the "one hundred to twenty to four" equation, and then consider that those four "still standing" believers will attend one of 300,000 churches in the United States, 95 percent of which are not producing disciplers. From this, we can conclude that *there is almost no chance for the remaining "four" to eventually become disciplers.*

Yes, that's zero!

The American church has buildings, small groups, staff, and programs, and all those are needed. But enduring one-to-one disciplemaking is missing.

Sustainable Discipleship Is Implicit

Disciplemaking becomes implicit when it's a practice that happens naturally. Put a discipler in a country that has no other believers, and that discipler will start discipling. It's part of who they are.

They'll constantly be asking the question, "Have you been discipled?" Well, perhaps they'll first pray, develop a relationship, and lead a person to the Lord. But then will come the question!

Implicit discipleship becomes a life discipline even during persecution. If a church loses the ability to meet in buildings and small groups are outlawed, then disciplers can still disciple one-to-one.

Hopefully, most of us will always have a church building to enter and a small group to attend, but what happens if we don't?

I've already mentioned that I've been to Russia dozens of times. When we first arrived in the early 1990s, Russia had been seventy years without an evangelical church structure—no pastors, seminaries, publishing houses, church buildings, or small groups.

Nothing. New believers didn't even have a heritage of remembering Christian parents or grandparents.

When we first started going to Russia, there were no believers, so we held evangelistic crusades. When many accepted Jesus, and there were no pastors, we trained pastors. When there were both believers and pastors, we planted churches.

From crusades to pastors to churches! We also began training in discipleship. We called our mission organization *Russians Reaching Russians*. From the first trip in 1992, we knew that any future trip could be our last.

With the mindset of "this could be our last trip," we continued with church planting, leadership development, and disciplemaking training for thirty years. We told our Russian friends, "Hey, this could be our last trip, and you must learn to be faithful without us."

We wanted the fruit of our mission organization to be literally *Russians Reaching Russians!*

My last trip to Russia was in November 2019. As I sat waiting to board my plane, I admit I didn't think, *This could be my last trip*. But then came COVID-19 and Russia's military operation in Ukraine, and the reality hit me: maybe it *was* my last trip.

I know many pastors and Christian leaders in Russia, and I've been unable to have in-depth communication with them. I've received cryptic emails in which they report, "We are doing okay," but that's been all.

Until recently.

A woman involved in ministry in the St. Petersburg area traveled to Ohio and gave me a message from one of the Russian pastors. The message was, "Tell Pastor Grant this is what is happening in Russia: Russians are reaching Russians!"

Disciplemaking is now implicit in the lives of many believers in Russia!

Let's Reposition

At the beginning of this chapter, I mentioned that I tell those who ask about my retirement that I've not retired, just repositioned myself to encourage the development of a discipling culture in churches.

Few churches in America have one. They have large and small group gatherings but little one-to-one disciplemaking.

Please note: I'm not against large churches (I've pastored one), nor am I against small groups (having been a member of one for forty years). But I see what I hope you're also seeing—a desperate need to add one-to-one disciplemaking to the mix.

The church needs large gatherings, small gatherings, *and* one-to-one discipleship!

For that to happen—for churches to develop a shared, pervasive, enduring, and implicit culture of disciplemaking—churches need to reposition by asking the question . . .

"Have you been discipled?"

To review: Disciplemaking works when there is correct content, culture, and connections. In Chapter 7, we considered content. In this chapter, we tackled culture, and in Chapter 9, we'll explore connections.

> **Churches need to reposition by asking the question . . . "Have you been discipled?"**

Then, in the closing chapters of this book, we'll look at practical ways to reposition your church to embrace disciplemaking.

So keep reading! The best chapters are still to come!

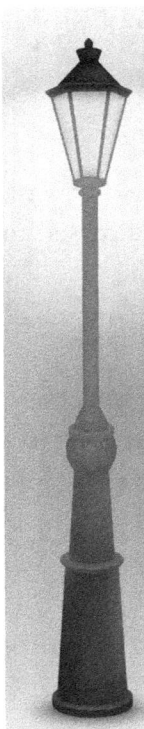

Review:
- LampPost Rule #1: Admit the problem.
- LampPost Rule #2: Know the right definition and content.
- LampPost Rule #3: Understand the blueprint.
- LampPost Rule #4: Know best practices.
- LampPost Rule #5: I can do this!
- LampPost Rule #6: Implement *The LampPost Strategy*.
- LampPost Rule #7: Foundation to Calling to Formation.
- LampPost Rule #8: Have you been discipled?

Gain confidence in your ability to make disciples by reading the testimony in *Interlude #8*.

Interlude #8:

You Can Do This!

Diana's Story

I was raised in a home that believed in God, and I was taught the difference between good and bad.

But I didn't know God and His character.

I lived only for myself for thirty years. I went to church and looked like a Christian but didn't really have a relationship with Jesus. I kept trying to fill this empty spot in my life by trying to be a good person.

I wasn't successful in my attempts to be good, and I continued having sin infect every part of my life. And all of this while I was attending church regularly.

Then I was asked to be discipled.

At first, I didn't think that I needed to be discipled, but I was asked by a woman whom I respected for her walk with Jesus. During our discipling process, for the first time, I understood God's grace and that I could have a personal relationship with Jesus.

I look back on my discipleship now and wish that I could have been discipled when I first started to attend church. I would not have suffered the consequences of sin in my life and would have experienced the freedom that I found in Jesus at a much earlier age.

I now have a passion for discipling others, which is why I invited Donna to go through *First Steps* with me.

Donna's Story

I was one of five children.

My early childhood home was dysfunctional, and I suffered abuse. Like many children who suffer abuse, I felt that I was somehow responsible for my parents' abusive behavior.

After high school, I knew that I had to leave home, so I joined the Air Force. While the Air Force provided structure for my life professionally, my personal life fell apart. I found myself divorced and moving from one bad relationship to another.

I was suicidal when a friend asked me to attend church. I attended infrequently and wasn't getting what I needed to establish my faith.

Then my friend Diana, who led a Bible study in which I participated, called and asked if I wanted to be discipled. I didn't really understand what "be discipled" meant but I still said "yes."

We went through *First Steps Conversations* together.

It was ten weeks of wonderful study and conversations about Jesus, and I learned that God loves me! I guess I should have known this, but in our discipleship, our conversations about Jesus made Him real in a way that I had never experienced before.

I also learned that I could pray to Jesus and ask Him specific requests and how to build a solid foundation for my faith.

Probably the first chapter in *First Steps* was the most influential.

In this chapter, I understood that Jesus could change my life, and my doubt evaporated about a Jesus who loved me. I was able to leave my guilt from the past and enjoy the freedom that can only be found by following Jesus.

Discipleship changed my life.

I thank Diana for taking the time to invite me into a discipling relationship.

Chapter 9:

Making the Connection

Christianity without the living Christ is inevitably Christianity without discipleship, and Christianity without discipleship is always Christianity without Christ.[21]

For effective discipleship, a discipler must connect with a disciple. The inability to make a connection between a person wanting to disciple and someone needing to be discipled is a major reason for failure in disciplemaking. However, "making the connection" is complicated and not easily implemented.

Let me explain two reasons for this.

- Trained disciplers do not naturally look for someone to disciple. I often hear this question: "I'm ready to disciple; now give me the name of a person to disciple."

  If a church or an organization permanently accepts the primary responsibility for connecting a discipler with a disciple, sooner or later, there will be more disciplers than disciples.

  And with no one to disciple, those being trained and wanting to disciple will lose enthusiasm.

- Churches don't organize correctly for disciplemaking. A church must plan disciplemaking to develop disciplers who find their *own* disciples.

    This is "bottom-up" organizing, not "top-down" promotion. It's practically impossible to suddenly develop a large group of disciplers and keep them motivated and connected to disciples.

    The best approach is to start with a small group of disciplers, allowing their success to challenge others to disciple.

    Again, bottom-up organizing not top-down promotion.

Training small numbers and allowing slow growth is juxtaposed with building big and desiring quick growth. One-to-one discipleship requires a slow growth approach, while projects like building a new sanctuary need a faster response.

We're wired to want to see big results fast, which is fine if you're trying to raise money to build a new sanctuary. But disciplemaking initially requires a slower pace, one that will increase as more and more disciples become disciplemakers. Exponential growth *will* take place (two disciples will become four, those four will become eight, then sixteen, and so on), but you'll need to be patient.

And it's worth being patient.

A Review of the Three C's

There are three C's for successful discipleship—Content, Culture, and Connections.

Content Review:

New believers need foundational discipleship in the first three months. It's essential to have the right content that develops the four foundational disciplines and anticipates the similar temptations or growth areas that all new believers experience.

And that content must be shaped so a discipler will believe, "I can use this material. I can do this!"

Culture Review:

A sustainable culture of discipleship in a local church should be shared, pervasive, enduring, and implicit. A church has buildings, programs, staff, and other activities, and all are important—but none are as central to responding to the cause of Christ as making disciples.

One question indicates a church or organization that has a culture of disciplemaking: "Have you been discipled?"

Now, let's consider the last C, *Connection:*

For successful disciplemaking, disciplers must be connected to a disciple. The goal of "connection" is developing disciplers who find their own disciples to disciple.

The mindset of a disciplemaker should be, "I'm responsible for finding someone to disciple. God, bring me someone to disciple."

A Car Salesman's Responsibility

My father was a used car salesman, so I grew up hearing lots of conversations about sales.

As a car salesman, my dad's primary concern was selling a car. Why? My father worked only on commission, and no sales meant no money.

My dad worked long hours but was always home to eat with the family. During dinner, we often asked, "Dad, did you sell any cars today?" "Yes" meant good times for us, and "No" meant the opposite.

In middle school, I learned to ask my father for a new pair of shoes—or some other extremely important item needed for whatever I thought was extremely important at the time—only when he'd been selling a lot of cars.

I kept a weekly tally of how many cars he'd sold because I knew if he hadn't sold a car that week, I couldn't ask for anything. If he'd sold one or two cars that week, I kept my requests minimal. But if he'd sold three to six cars during the week, I asked for the big stuff!

One day, I asked my dad, "What is the best way to sell cars?" My father answered, "You have to connect the right customer to the right car." If my dad had a great car but no one to purchase the car, then there would be no sale. If he had a customer wanting a specific car and that car wasn't on the car lot, then there was no sale either.

It was a simple rule of supply and demand.

The right customer had to be connected to the right car right then or the sale collapsed. Even if my dad waited a day to find the right customer for a car or the right car for a customer, the sale often fell apart.

My questions about my father's sales grew more intense in high school. With sports, dating, and the used car I owned needing repairs, I wanted my dad to sell lots of cars!

At dinner one night, my dad was describing a new car with low mileage that had become available that day. Realizing his need to connect a customer to this car, I asked him, "Where will you find a customer?"

His simple response was, "That's my responsibility."

Those are words disciplers need to own too. The Great Commission teaches us to "Go therefore and make disciples!" but for that to happen successfully, disciplers need to be responsible for finding disciples.

It's a simple rule of supply and demand.

This is LampPost Rule #9: God, bring me someone to disciple.

Supply and Demand

A new believer who's not discipled will walk away from faithfulness in the first three months. A discipler trained and motivated to disciple, without finding someone to disciple, will walk away from discipling.

The church today has two problems with disciplemaking, both the result of breaking the law of supply and demand: new believers walking away from faithfulness because disciplers aren't available and disciplers walking away from disciplemaking because there's no one to disciple.

I've taught Saturday conferences on disciplemaking and had hundreds of people stand to make a commitment to disciple one person a year . . . but they don't do it.

The reason? No one to disciple.

I know a church that had four hundred accept Jesus one Sunday, and then 95 percent walked away within three months. This church didn't have four hundred trained disciplers. Jesus knew about the law of supply and demand when He taught about workers in the harvest.

> *The harvest is plentiful, but the laborers are few; therefore beseech the Lord of the harvest to send out laborers into His harvest.* (Luke 10:2, NASB1995)

We should pray for revival.

But why pray for revival when there are no disciplers? Revival without disciplemaking leaves fresh fruit rotting in a field.

A church or organization desiring successful discipleship must have a plan for making connections between disciplers and disciples. There are two strategies that solve the problem of supply and demand.

First, developing 3rd generation disciplers.

Second, motivating disciplers.

3rd Generation Disciplers

I was discussing discipleship with a friend.

We wondered why many believers, though confessing Jesus as Lord and Savior, didn't obey Jesus to go and make disciplers.

I told my friend, "We need disciplers, not disciples."

He said:

> *I agree, and let me tell you a story about when I worked in a blood donor organization. I noticed most of those who gave blood once never came back. Some would, but most would not.*

I wanted to know what it would take to turn those first-time donors into committed blood donors. I did my homework and discovered two things:

First, if someone sat with a first-time donor and processed their experience with them, they tended to come back. Even if the first-timer was stuck several times by a technician who never found a vein, if they were reaffirmed of the value of their willingness to donate and help others, they often came back to try again.

Second, I found that if the person came back three times, that person then transformed from someone who donated blood if it was convenient to someone who thought of themselves as a blood donor—and they'd seek out opportunities to donate. They wanted that one-gallon pin and then the two- and three-gallon pins.

Donating blood became a part of who they were. They didn't just give blood; they were blood donors and proud of it.

When my friend finished his blood donor story, I thought, "The church needs blood donor-style disciplers, not just disciples."

I mentioned Dr. Ron Braley earlier in this book. He has a PhD in the analytics of spiritual formation with believers. He recently told me, *"My research indicates that the solution to the supply and demand problem of disciplemaking in the church is that we must take consumers and make them disciples and then take the disciples and make them disciplers."*

The Apostle Paul wrote to Timothy:

> *The things which you have heard from me in the presence of many witnesses, entrust these to faithful men who will be able to teach others also.* (2 Timothy 2:2, NASB1995)

When I observed disciplemaking, I noticed a pattern. If a follower is discipled and then disciples two others—their passion for discipleship becomes a defining characteristic of walking with Jesus.

What Is a 3rd Generation Discipler?

A 3rd generation discipler will seek out someone to disciple.

They're believers who've been discipled (first generation), who successfully discipled another with coaching (second generation), and who then successfully discipled another by themselves (third generation).

> "A 3rd generation discipler will seek out someone to disciple."

My disciples become 3rd generation disciplers when I disciple them, work with them in their first disciplemaking matchup (often attending sessions with them), and continue to coach and pray in their first solo disciplemaking adventure.

It's great when God works through me and even better when I observe God working through someone that I discipled.

Third generation disciplers find joy in disciplemaking and look for people to disciple. It becomes their identity!

I know many 3rd generation disciplers with similar characteristics:

- They develop confidence, believing, "I can do this!"
- They frequently ask others, "Have you been discipled?"
- They often tell their disciples, "You can do this!"
- They pray, "God, bring me someone to disciple."

Paul writes:

> *Therefore, my dear brothers and sisters, stay true to the Lord. I love you and long to see you, dear friends, for you are my joy and the crown I receive for my work.* (Philippians 4:1, NLT)

With 3rd generation disciplers, the problem of supply and demand disappears as disciplers find their own disciples to disciple.

Like I used to ask for "big stuff" from my car salesman father, let's ask our Father in heaven for someone to disciple.

God always answers this prayer.

Motivating 3rd Generation Disciplers

Love is the greatest motive.

We can't talk ourselves into loving more. If we get up one morning and think, *I'm going to be a more loving person today*, it won't work. Growing in love requires action from us.

The lasting motive for disciplemaking is love—we disciple because we love to disciple.

However, we can't wake up one morning and think, *I'm going to love being a discipler*. We have to actually disciple, and through disciplemaking, our love for discipling grows.

As John writes:

> *For this is the love of God, that we keep His commandments; and His commandments are not burdensome.* (1 John 5:3, NASB1995)

Disciplemaking motivated by love can't be stopped. It overcomes discipleship inertia and brings about sustainable disciplemaking. A follower of Jesus who has learned the power of command-obey-love will think, *Who can I disciple next?*

Third generation disciplers are motivated by love.

The Love of Disciplemaking

In the early 2000s, a prisoner in an Ohio prison came to know Jesus.

His life was radically changed, and when he heard that a national organization was going to hold an evangelism rally in his prison, he began praying that many of the inmates at his prison would come to know Jesus as Lord and Savior.

When he learned he'd been granted early release on parole three weeks before the rally, he went to the prison authorities and asked that his sentence be extended by three weeks.

They agreed, but the news of a prisoner wanting his sentence to be increased was reported in newspapers.

The family of the victim of his crime heard about his early release and filed a complaint with prison authorities. In response to this complaint, his early parole was revoked, and instead of a three-week extension, he was required to serve the rest of his sentence of three more years.

From three weeks to three years because he wanted to be involved in a crusade at his prison.

After the evangelistic rally, I held a discipleship conference in that prison. He attended the three-day conference, and afterward, he said to me, "I believe that becoming a discipler in this prison is the reason that I had my sentence extended by three years."

A few months later, I was back at the prison for another disciple-making training. He attended and afterward mentioned that he was discipling five inmates. I reminded him that he was asked in the training to only disciple one person per year.

He said, "Hey, I'm in prison; what else am I going to do?"

Capacity for Disciplemaking and Testing God

A church's capacity for sustained disciplemaking is equivalent to the number of its disciplers. A church with 100 disciplemakers can disciple 100 new or renewed believers. If 200, then 200, if 300, then 300, and imagine a church with 1,000 or 10,000 disciplers.

Considering the law of supply and demand of disciplers and disciples, 3rd generation disciplers are essential. They are motivated by love to find others to disciple.

But what's the best way to find a disciple?

In 1974, I tested a theory about overcoming the law of supply and demand with disciplemaking. I asked God to place people on my heart who needed to know Jesus as their Lord and, after accepting Jesus, would need to be discipled.

Eventually, I developed a list of thirty-five people. I prayed for them to find Jesus and to be discipled. I knew that God probably wanted to answer my prayers more than I wanted to ask the prayers.

I also realized that I was testing God, which was forbidden in the Old Testament (Deuteronomy 6:16), but since the prophet Malachi allowed testing for tithes and offerings (Malachi 3:10), I figured that God wouldn't mind my test case of thirty-five people with disciplemaking.

What happened?

Two years later, thirty-three of the thirty-five "test case" participants were following Jesus and had been discipled.

Those on the list were unknowing participants of my test case. With some, I was active in discussions about salvation and discipleship, but with others I just prayed.

A young lady came to our ministry one evening, and I felt a nudge to place her on the list. She accepted Jesus and was discipled. A year later, this young woman brought her sister to a meeting at our ministry. I didn't place the sister on the list but did pray for her—fervently prayed for her. This sister did come to know Jesus, was discipled, and eventually became my wife.

As the Apostle Paul writes:

> *Now to Him who is able to do far more abundantly beyond all that we ask or think.* (Ephesians 3:20, NASB1995)

A 3rd generation discipler has the attitude of, "Who will I disciple next?" I have never heard of a discipler asking for someone to disciple without the Lord answering the prayer.

Organizing Connections

If releasing 3rd generation disciplers is the goal in a church, there needs to be a process for developing, encouraging, and training disciplers. But first, a revolution is needed to overcome the discipleship inertia with believers.

That's the next chapter: revolution!

Chapter 9: Making the Connection

Review:
- LampPost Rule #1: Admit the problem.
- LampPost Rule #2: Know the right definition and content.
- LampPost Rule #3: Understand the blueprint.
- LampPost Rule #4: Know best practices.
- LampPost Rule #5: I can do this!
- LampPost Rule #6: Implement *The LampPost Strategy*.
- LampPost Rule #7: Foundation to Calling to Formation.
- LampPost Rule #8: Have you been discipled?
- LampPost Rule #9: God, bring me someone to disciple.

For discipleship to work, we must understand and solve the law of supply and demand, discussed further in *Interlude #9*.

Interlude #9:

Law of Supply and Demand

And he said to them, "The harvest is plentiful, but the laborers are few. Therefore pray earnestly to the Lord of the harvest to send out laborers into his harvest. (Luke 10:2, ESV)

There are disciplers, and there are also those needing to be discipled. Jesus didn't ask His followers in the first century to pray for an increase in the size of the crowd following Him, but for workers to be sent into the harvest. When Jesus said we should pray for workers in the harvest, He was practicing what has become known as the law of supply and demand.

It's a simple law to understand.

If there are many who want to disciple and not enough people to be discipled, the disciplers will be frustrated and perhaps stop discipling. If there are many needing to be discipled and no one to disciple them, we get about 80 percent of new believers walking away from faithfulness.

For disciplemaking to work correctly, there must be a balance between disciplers and those who are willing to be discipled. That's the law of supply and demand in action.

The most productive disciplers are 3rd generation disciplers. The only way to flip the 80 percent walk-away rate to keeping 80 percent is to develop 3rd generation disciplers, believers who are willing to live by the following statement, question, and prayer:

- I can disciple!
- Do you want to be discipled?
- God, bring me someone to disciple.

Recently, I was talking to a former inmate whom I discipled while he was in an Ohio correctional institution. Since he understood the statement, question, and prayer, he told that me that he asked God to bring him someone to disciple.

Later, as he walked the hallways of his prison, two inmates approached him and asked to be discipled! The Holy Spirit evened the scales of supply and demand: men who wanted to be discipled and a discipler willing to disciple them.

Chapter 10:

Revolution

Jesus told us explicitly what to do. We have a manual, just like the car owner. He told us, as disciples, to make disciples.[22]

How victorious could an army be without foot soldiers trained with a willingness to follow their leader's commands?

Jesus was given all authority in heaven and on earth, and He then told His followers to make disciples. This disciplemaking command can't be misinterpreted to mean only "be disciples" or even to "plant and build churches." Jesus gave an easy analysis with the Great Commission—are we making disciples?

Yes or no?

The revolution of the Kingdom of God is releasing disciplemakers to teach the nations all that Jesus has commanded us.

Disciplers having the confidence to say, "I can do this!" Followers with sensitive boldness ask, "Have you been discipled?" Both are the intended results when Jesus gave His disciples the Great Commission.

Disciplers discipling disciplers is revolutionary.

Dallas Willard, one of the recent great authors on disciplemaking, wrote:

> *Once we who are disciples have assisted others with becoming disciples (of Jesus, not of us), we can gather them, in ordinary life situations, under the supernatural Trinitarian Presence, forming a new kind of social unit never before seen on earth.*[23]

And Willard continues:

> *It is a tragic error to think that Jesus was telling us, as he left, to start churches, as that is understood today. From time to time starting a church may be appropriate. But his aim for us is much greater than that. He wants us to establish "beachheads" or bases of operation for the Kingdom of God wherever we are.*[24]

Jesus meant for us to be radical. Following His command, all believers should become one-to-one disciplemakers. Filled with His Spirit, we can change the world. Jesus said to all of us:

> *But you will receive power when the Holy Spirit has come upon you; and you shall be My witnesses both in Jerusalem, and in all Judea and Samaria, and even to the remotest part of the earth.* (Acts 1:8, NASB1995)

Revolution!

Releasing individual disciplemakers as the primary vision of a local church is rarely found today. There is discipleship inertia, with churches distracted by programs, staff, and buildings and not focusing on disciplemaking.

How do we change? How do we move from church members to disciples and from disciples to disciplemakers?

We need a revolution.

Let's consider the revolutionary ideas discussed so far in this book:

- Jesus commanded all believers to become disciplemakers.
- New believers can be effective disciplers.

- There is a simple foundational disciplemaking plan for all believers.
- The best disciplemaking is one-to-one.
- All believers should have the confidence to say, "I can do this!"
- A culture of disciplemaking asks the question, "Have you been discipled?"
- Disciplers should pray, "God, bring me someone to disciple."

Disciplemaking is often discussed by Christian leaders, but these conversations lack the revolutionary ideas needed for exponential discipleship.

Jesus said:

> *And no one puts new wine into old wineskins; otherwise the new wine will burst the skins and it will be spilled out, and the skins will be ruined.* (Luke 5:37, NASB1995)

We need a new wineskin of disciplemaking.

A wineskin that understands how foundational discipleship works and how to implement it in a local church. Starting one-to-one discipling is not a top-down program and not a three-month lesson plan for small groups. It is bottom to top, small to large, and a few disciplers to many disciplers.

Revolutions start small.

Consider Jesus and the Twelve—a movement that overtook the Roman Empire and changed the world. In his book, *The Patient Ferment of the Early Church*, Alan Kreider cites sources that claim Christianity grew in the first three centuries by 40 percent per decade.[25]

I'm borrowing the title of Kreider's book to say that disciplemaking is started and maintained by a patient ferment.

Elements of a Disciplemaking Revolution

How do we create a discipling revolution in churches today? How do we start and sustain discipleship? How do we get the patient ferment of disciplemaking?

By planting a mustard seed:

> *Jesus said, "How can I describe the Kingdom of God? What story should I use to illustrate it? It is like a mustard seed planted in the ground. It is the smallest of all seeds, but it becomes the largest of all garden plants; it grows long branches, and birds can make nests in its shade."* (Mark 4:30–32, NLT)

Starting with a few committed disciplers, disciplemaking can grow to be the most influential ministry of any church. Disciplers discipling disciplers will provide the foundation for significant spiritual maturity and, eventually, exponential numerical growth.

It only takes a few determined disciplers to turn around disciplemaking inertia in a church or mission.

A few years back, I asked myself this question: "How many disciplers does it take to create a 'tipping point' for discipleship to become the major influence in a local church?"

> **How many disciplers does it take to create a "tipping point" in a local church?**

Those who read business books know that the phrase "tipping point" was used in Malcolm Gladwell's book entitled . . . wait for it:

The Tipping Point: How Little Things Can Make a Big Difference. As Gladwell explains:

> *This possibility of sudden change is at the center of the idea of the Tipping Point. . . . The Tipping Point is the moment of critical mass, the threshold, the boiling point.*[26]

That's the question. How do we reach the tipping point for disciple-making in a local church? How many disciplers does it take? My solution for a tipping-point revolution for disciplemaking became specific when I watched a 2013 TEDx from Boulder, Colorado.

In this talk, Erica Chenoweth described her study of revolutions. She had examined every revolution since the early 1900s. As I listened to this talk, I jotted down the following quotes:

> *Researchers used to say that no government could survive if just 5 percent of the population rose up against it.*
>
> *Our data showed that the number may be lower than that. . . .*
>
> *No single campaign has failed during that time period (from the early 1900s forward) after they had achieved the active and sustained participation of just 3.5 percent of the population, and a lot achieved success with far fewer than that.*
>
> *In the US today, that's like 11 million people.*

Erica Chenoweth also wrote a book titled *Civil Resistance* about her studies. In this book, she discusses her research of 637 revolutionary campaigns, and she adds a few points about revolution that are helpful when considering how to create a disciplemaking culture in a local church.

- The ideas undergirding revolution were already in the minds of people before the actual revolution.
- Revolutions that rely on nonviolent means are far more successful and long-lasting. Great news for disciplemaking in local churches!

A very small number can have a great impact.

That's LampPost Rule #10: A revolution starts small.

We don't need to be rude or condemn all the activities in churches. It's not necessary to make an entire congregation feel guilty because they aren't discipling. One-to-one disciplemaking is not a revolt against small groups, church buildings, or large church staff.

It is an addition.

Just as discipling is best one-to-one, developing discipleship as a major part of a local church is also one-to-one. One discipler to one disciple, then two individual disciplers to two individual disciples, then four individual disciplers to four individual disciples, and the exponential curve becomes unstoppable.

We just need to get 3.5 to 5 percent of a church's membership involved in disciplemaking, and disciplers will take over the church by undergirding every ministry, outreach, and worship service.

We need a revolution of obeying Jesus and His Great Commission. The idea of disciplemaking, already in the minds and hearts of millions of believers, just needs a workable strategy, a strategy found in Scripture from the parable of Jesus about the mustard seed.

3.5 to 5 Percent Mustard Seeds

I had just spoken at church on disciplemaking when a young man approached me. He told me that he had been attending this church for about three weeks. I asked him, "Have you been discipled?"

"No," he replied, "but I want to be."

I looked around the sanctuary to find someone to disciple him. Not seeing a discipler, I asked him to go to a table where the church's Disciple Connector was available to connect disciplers with disciples.

I then took my microphone back to the sound guy, and when I handed him the mic, I asked, "Would you like to disciple someone?" He immediately replied, "Yes!" I then walked him over to the young man and introduced them.

Later, the sound guy came up to me and said, "As you were speaking today, I felt conviction that I should disciple someone. And then you came up and asked me to disciple someone. That's why I gave an immediate 'yes.'"

When 3.5 to 5 percent of the membership of a local church begins to say, "I can do this!" and ask the question, "Do you want to be discipled?"—that's an unstoppable revolution!

A church does not have to train dozens of disciplemakers at one time. To be honest, I don't think a church should even try. Start smaller!

When discussing percentages of membership, I believe a smaller church needs a higher percentage. And in a larger church, perhaps 5 percent is too much. In the next chapter, I discuss that every church should try for twelve to start a discipling ministry.

But regardless of the percentage, with a very small number giving testimony of the effectiveness of one-to-one disciplemaking, a church's culture will change.

A discipling revolution isn't about firing pastors or shuttering large buildings to make room for disciplemaking. Disciplemaking starts small and slowly adds more disciplers until it can't be quenched.

A one-to-one discipling revolution can quickly overwhelm discipleship inertia.

Something else, though . . .

A Revolution Needs a Focal Point

I was part of the Hippie Movement. We had a focal point—we were against the war in Vietnam.

We had the slogan, "Make love, not war." We were anti-system and wanted to drop out of the establishment. When the Vietnam War ended, the focus of my generation's impetus for revolt went away.

Going back to college, starting families, or taking jobs in big corporations, we sold out to the system that we once opposed. There was no longer a focal point for rebellion.

Toward the end of the Hippie Movement, something else began. Known as the Jesus Revolution, in the latter 1960s and early 1970s, millions of young people began following Jesus.

I became a believer during the Jesus Movement, and the 80 percent walk-away rate happened with those millions of believers. Why? No discipleship.

It's why I pray for a disciplemaking revolution. Disciplemaking has been lost in the church. And most attempts at disciplemaking still sputter without a replicable focal point.

That focal point is foundational disciplemaking.

> **That focal point is foundational disciplemaking.**

The greatest harm to discipleship has been the false idea that following the command of Jesus is a "figure it out," "many ways to disciple," or "we already have small groups" paths to discipling.

One-to-one disciplemaking needs to become a revolution. With only 3.5 to 5 percent of the members of a church, with only 3.5 to 5 percent of a city's population, and with only 3.5 to 5 percent of the population of the USA needed—we can start a revolution.

As hippies used to say, "Power to the people!"

Sustaining a Revolution

An event that changed the world happened on December 17, 1903, when Orville Wright piloted an aircraft to 853 feet in 59 seconds. Our world has never been the same.

Looking out a window in an airport terminal, we can see many types of aircraft, from an Airbus A350 soon departing for Europe to a Cessna 172 flying to the next state, and all these aircraft use the same design that the Wright brothers used in building their first flying machine.

The revolution of flight continues to impact the world.

There are two stories behind the first airplane. The first is known by everyone, and the second is unknown to most.

First: how two brothers, lacking college educations, who owned a bike shop, managed to figure out the principles of flight and then design an airplane that could fly. It's a legendary story that still inspires.

Second: how they received credit for their inventions through the patents developed by a lawyer who practiced in Springfield, Ohio. This story, just as important, lies buried in the annals of the revolution of flight.

The Wright Brothers

The story of Orville and Wilbur Wright illustrates the importance of hard work, endurance, perseverance, amazing insights, great skill, sheer luck, divine providence, and any other words or phrases depicting perspiration and overcoming the odds that might be used.

Let's consider what Orville and Wilbur invented.

They developed the first stabilized, powered, heavier-than-air flying machine by discovering the foundations of aeronautical engineering. Their new technology included the revolutionary design of rudders, ailerons, and flaps.

Without which, no plane can fly.

Though flying had been discussed for thousands of years, before the 1900s, there was little practical knowledge about actual flying, either with a glider or powered flight. Orville Wright has been quoted as saying, "We had to go ahead and discover everything for ourselves."

Skepticism abounded about the possibility of flight. David McCullough, who wrote the bestselling book *The Wright Brothers*, describes Bill Tate, a man from the Outer Banks who helped assemble one of the Wright brothers' first gliders in Kitty Hawk, as saying:

> "Outer Banks people were still pretty set in their ways."
>
> Tate added, "We believed in a good God, a bad Devil, and a hot Hell, and more than anything else, we believed that same God did not intend man should ever fly."[27]

Wilbur and Orville Wright learned the aerodynamics of flying, how to control an airplane during flight, and how to power the plane. They had little guidance from the past, and with others being killed in their attempts at flying, the Wright brothers moved forward with small steps, experimenting and practicing, with an eye toward safety and ultimate success.

They knew they must learn to pilot an aircraft when an actual airplane to fly didn't yet exist. The Wright brothers literally accomplished the amazing feat of building a plane while flying it!

The brothers designed gliders and flew them—knowing they could be killed each time a glider left the ground. Once they gained in-flight control of a glider, they needed to develop an engine and propellers to power a plane for sustained flight.

While other inventors benefited from the investment of tens of thousands of dollars from industrialists and even governments, the Wright brothers' successful "Wright Flyer" only cost about $1,000 to build.

And it was their money.

There were so many failed attempts at building a powered airplane that the impossibility of flying grew more entrenched in most people's minds. Often mocked and ridiculed, the Wright brothers endured until December 17, 1903, when all their time, effort, ingenuity, and money came together for the first powered flight.

Yet, for a couple of years after 1903, skepticism about the possibility of flying kept most from noticing or believing the news from Kitty Hawk. But when belief began to grow, Wilbur and Orville faced another problem—others stealing their ideas.

Harry A. Toulmin

From the office where I am writing this book, I can look out my window and see the building where the Wright brothers filed the patents for their aeronautical inventions.

I have known this for years.

Chapter 10: Revolution

I pass this building on the way to my favorite coffee shop. Set in front of the building is a bronze statue of a man holding a cigar. It seemed odd that our city leaders would deem it acceptable to immortalize smoking.

That was my thinking until one morning when I stopped to read a sign next to the statue. It said the statue commemorated Harry A. Toulmin. I also noticed it's not a cigar he's holding but a pen, signifying his work as a patent attorney.

I didn't know this until I read the sign.

Many institutions and places in my area are named for the Wright brothers. We have Wright-Patterson Air Force Base, Wright State University, the Wright Brothers National Museum, and Wright-Patt Credit Union. But nothing is named after Harry A. Toulmin. Yet, if it wasn't for Attorney Toulmin, the Wright brothers may never have been fully credited with inventing the airplane.

Anticipating eventual challenges to their inventions, the Wright brothers traveled to Springfield, Ohio, in 1904 to hire Harry A. Toulmin as their patent attorney. Toulmin quickly discerned that a patent shouldn't be filed on the Wright brothers' plane but on the control systems for their airplane.

Harry Toulmin wrote US Patent No. 821.393, giving the Wright brothers solitary claim to the only control system ever built or used for controlling an airplane in the air. As you study this brilliant patent by Toulmin, you realize that it gave patent authority to the Wrights for things like rudders, ailerons, stabilizers, and flaps.

Again, look through the window of that departure terminal window and realize that an Airbus A350 and Cessna 172 both have flaps, rudders, stabilizers, and ailerons, or technology developed by the Wright brothers and patented by Harry A. Toulmin.

The Wright brothers developed the fundamentals of flight, and Harry Toulmin helped them define and understand their inventions so they could be patented.

The Wright brothers and Toulmin didn't follow the "there are many ways to fly" philosophy. There were many that tried this approach before the Wright brothers, only to crash. Airplanes, no matter what they look like today, still follow the same foundational principles of aeronautical design.

Could this be the reason that discipleship hasn't worked? The fundamentals of Christian maturity haven't been known and applied to new believers.

A Revolution in Disciplemaking

There's much discussion about discipleship today, often from a publishing or scholastic perspective, with little supporting practical experience. Unfortunately, with the resultant failed attempts at disciplemaking, there can be a growing antipathy about the ability of the American church to make disciples.

I keep trying; let's keep trying.

I know that the principles of this book work individually with new believers. I am still developing an understanding of creating a culture of disciplemaking in local churches, communities, and missions.

With disciplemaking, sometimes we find victory, and sometimes unexpected forces cause frustration. The Wright brothers' first flying machine was soon upended by an errant wind gust while it sat on the ground, and it never flew again.

But understanding the correct foundation of disciplemaking gives us the possibility of success beyond imagination.

I wonder what Wilbur Wright, on that first flight, lying prone on wings of sewn muslin, would think today if he boarded a Boeing 787 Dreamliner to sit in first class on a seat that turned into a bed?

We've discussed the foundations of disciplemaking in this book and the need for a revolution in discipleship. In the next chapters, I will discuss what I've learned about establishing LampPost communities of disciplemaking.

If we can be successful, others will notice.

The seemingly impossible will happen too—as 80 percent stay committed instead of walking away from faithfulness.

Review:
- LampPost Rule #1: Admit the problem.
- LampPost Rule #2: Know the right definition and content.
- LampPost Rule #3: Understand the blueprint.
- LampPost Rule #4: Know best practices.
- LampPost Rule #5: I can do this!
- LampPost Rule #6: Implement *The LampPost Strategy*.
- LampPost Rule #7: Foundation to Calling to Formation.
- LampPost Rule #8: Have you been discipled?
- LampPost Rule #9: God, bring me someone to disciple.
- LampPost Rule #10: A revolution starts small.

What does Albert Einstein have to do with disciplemaking? Find out by reading *Interlude #10*.

Interlude #10:

Albert Einstein and Disciplemaking

$E = mc^2$

Albert Einstein is legendary for conceptualizing the general theory of relativity. If you call someone "Einstein," you mean that the person is brilliant.

I've had a fascination with Einstein's theory for years and confess that I don't understand it at all. I know that Sir Isaac Newton and Albert Einstein both had theories of gravity that are seemingly contradictory.

Yet both theories have been proven to work within a certain framework. Scientists haven't been able to explain how two contradictory theories both work, and so they must sit beside me in the corner of a classroom wearing a dunce cap.

I wish Newton and Einstein could have lived in the same century so they could have boxed it out for victory in their respective theoretical universes.

We know in one area—how light bends around objects—that Einstein was right. This discovery has led to the explanation of things like nuclear energy, the big bang theory, and—if you run fast enough—you can live forever (so long as it's the speed of light).

The story of Albert Einstein's general theory of relativity involves two men—Albert Einstein and British astronomer Arthur Stanley Eddington.

Einstein finished his general theory of relativity in 1915.

At the time, he was unknown. With World War I raging, Eddington and Einstein did not meet during the war. But Eddington did understand the importance of Einstein's theory and realized (as an astronomer) that a solar eclipse expected on May 28, 1919, could prove Albert Einstein's general theory of relativity.

Arthur Eddington then took it upon himself, without Einstein knowing about it, to mount expeditions to two locations in differing parts of the world. During this upcoming eclipse, scientific instruments could measure the bending of light around the sun and prove or disprove the general theory of relativity.

Expeditions at that time were, to say the least, very difficult.

Traveling to different parts of the world, Eddington's expeditions would have to excite enough interest, with a world distracted by war, to raise the necessary funds, and then besides the typical hassles of traveling to remote parts of the globe, probably need to dodge a few German U-Boats on the way.

Fortunately, World War I ended in late 1918, and with the expedition a "go," the scientific data was collected.

When the results of Eddington's expeditions were presented on November 6, 1919, at the Royal Astronomical Society in London, Albert Einstein's general theory of relativity was proven to be correct. The president of the Royal Society then claimed that the general theory of relativity was the highest achievement of human thought.

Those who could understand this theory knew it was a complete revolution in science.

Let's remember, Einstein knew little of this. He was sick in bed from illnesses stemming from malnutrition during World War I when he heard the news of Eddington's successful tests.

Later, when Albert Einstein was asked how he would have reacted if Eddington's calculations had disproved his theory, he said, "I would have felt sorry for the dear Lord. The theory is correct."

Yes, disciplemaking is a stretch from Einstein.

I have written several times in this book that, whereas my Foundation-Calling-Formation theory works, I have few analyses about changing the culture of a church to discipling to prove my theory correct.

But I know it works because I've seen it work, and since it's the Lord's command, I know the church will be blessed.

I'm with Einstein on this: we don't have to feel sorry for God because the theory is correct.

We only have to feel sorry for the church if we, as the church, don't get busy with disciplemaking.

Chapter 11:

3rd Generation Disciplers

During a week of final exams, while I was in Bible college, someone gave me a copy of *The Lion, the Witch and the Wardrobe* by C. S. Lewis.

I love fantasy and science fiction books but had not heard of *The Chronicles of Narnia*. I sat down in the library of the Bible college and began to read. I was supposed to be studying for a Greek exam, but reading the story of Lucy finding an old wardrobe in the country house of an aged professor . . .

I couldn't put the book down.

As Lucy walked in and through the wardrobe, her arms stretched out in front of her, she first felt old clothing and then something like branches on trees. She kept going, realizing the wardrobe was larger than she had first thought.

As she walked, she heard something crunching beneath her feet. And in the distance, Lucy saw the first glimmers of light as she came through the wardrobe and into Narnia.

C. S. Lewis writes:

> *A moment later, she found that she was standing in the middle of a wood at night-time with snow under her feet and snowflakes falling through the air.*[28]

In the distance, Lucy saw the light. Intrigued, she kept walking:

> *In about ten minutes, she reached it and found it was a lamp post. As she stood looking at it, wondering why there was a lamp post in the middle of a wood and wondering what to do next . . .* [29]

This book discusses one-to-one disciplemaking. Like Lucy, are you wondering what to do next?

Because of Lucy and the Narnia lamppost, I didn't get a stellar grade on my Greek exam that semester. I did discover Narnia, Aslan, and the image of a lamppost in a dark place where something had gone considerably wrong.

Disciplemaking is the solution to the lack of spiritual maturity in the church today. It's a light in a dark place. It's the solution for something that's gone considerably wrong.

But as Lucy thought when first glimpsing the lamp post, "What to do next?"

Let's Establish a LampPost!

You want to disciple. You want disciplemaking to become part of your church's DNA. But perhaps you share Lucy's question: What to do next?

Answering that question is the point of this book: *Discipleship That Works: The LampPost Strategy for Disciplemaking*.

All disciplemaking should start with a foundation, but a foundation is useless without knowing what's being constructed—and why you're bothering to build at all. What is the goal of discipleship?

Let's review Paul's words to Timothy again:

> *The things which you have heard from me in the presence of many witnesses, entrust these to faithful men who will be able to teach others also.* (2 Timothy 2:2, NASB1995)

I've found that disciples who disciple have greater spiritual depth than non-disciplers. And while spiritual maturity is difficult to assess, it's easy to ask yourself and others these simple questions: "Am I discipling?" or "Are you discipling someone?"

Just as foundational discipleship must be kept simple and easy to learn so all believers can disciple and experience the Lord working through them to help others, disciplemaking in a church must be an easy-to-know and observable process.

The goal of one-to-one disciplemaking should produce disciplers who disciple disciplers. The purpose is not just to disciple or for a disciple to attempt discipling, but for followers of Jesus to become 3rd generation disciplers.

That's LampPost Rule #11: The goal is 3rd generation disciplers.

As mentioned in Chapter 9, a 3rd generation discipler has been discipled (1st generation), has discipled another while being mentored or coached (2nd generation), and has successfully "soloed" in discipling another (3rd generation).

A 3rd generation discipler has a high probability of becoming a discipler who believes, "I can do this!" who also asks others, "Have you been discipled?" and who prays, "God, bring me someone to disciple."

Discipling becomes a lifestyle for a 3rd generation disciplemaker. Place this discipler anywhere, and others will be discipled as disciplemaking is spread by passionate disciplers.

The objective of a LampPost is to gather 3rd generation disciplers. If we get one 3rd generation discipler, that's an accomplishment. If we get twenty, even better, but when 3.5 to 5 percent of a church is 3rd generation disciplers, we get a revolution.

How do we know if we have a successful LampPost? Ask the question, "How many 3rd generation disciplers are there?" Get a small percentage of 3rd generation disciplers in your church or your community, and there will be a tipping point of disciplemaking.

Never-Break Rules of a LampPost

Let me briefly review what I mean by a LampPost.

A LampPost is a community of disciplers who encourage one another to disciple disciplers.

Each LampPost community recognizes the need for foundational discipleship as the basis of everyone's formational calling. The community of disciplers can be a local church or a group of individuals from many churches working together. Since few churches are making disciplemakers, a LampPost will be a light in the darkness.

There are foundational principles with individuals wanting to begin one-to-one disciplemaking and with disciplemaking ministries in a church or community.

Below are five "Never-Break" rules for developing a LampPost.

By the way, after explaining the five Never-Break rules for organizing discipleship, I'll answer two questions: "What do I do next?" and "What should my church do next?"

Never-Break Rule #1: Small to large, and few to many!

Successful disciplemaking requires a commitment to starting small.

If a church hasn't actively pursued sustainable disciplemaking, there is no quick and easy programmatic fix.

A deliberate strategy of slow growth is essential. Expectations should not be large and quick but few and stable. Once a disciple develops a lifestyle of disciplemaking, this follower of Jesus will disciple over and over.

With many discipling again and again, disciplemaking will become an exponential juggernaut.

But it will start slowly and small—so expect that.

Never-Break Rule #2: Leaders must be examples!

I remember watching Ben Crenshaw win the Masters golf tournament in 1995 (I know, I'm old.).

As Crenshaw's putt went into the hole on the eighteenth green, he bent to his knees with emotion. While Ben Crenshaw was reacting to his victory, the television announcers described his difficult week at the Masters tournament because of the recent death of Crenshaw's mentor, Harvey Penick.

Knowing little about golf, I was intrigued by Harvey Penick. I found that Penick had written a book titled *Harvey Penick's Little Red Book*.

Penick's book was his diary. The book wasn't just ideas with "how-to" steps. Harvey Penick had spent his life teaching others how to swing a golf club, and every insight gained through years of instruction and learning was noted in his journal.

Penick's *Little Red Book* became an instant bestseller. Harvey Penick inspired other golfers because his teachings came from his life. He was an example.

From golf to disciplemaking, it won't happen unless leaders set an example.

Never-Break Rule #3: Focus on the relationship!

Everything about disciplemaking must elevate our relationship with Jesus. One-to-one discipleship focuses on experiencing Jesus in both truth and love.

> **From golf to disciplemaking, it won't happen unless leaders set an example.**

Love motivates our desire to draw closer and be faithful to God, and all our actions must come from our relationship with Him. We disciple because we know Jesus. We also pray, read the Bible, and are part of His body, the church—because we love Him.

And relationships are learned in relationships.

Early in my faith, I learned that when I draw near to God, He draws near to me (James 4:8). When I read my Bible and pray, I experience God and literally feel better. Because of my relationship with Jesus, I don't have difficulty with the discipline of daily devotions.

It's easy to do what we enjoy.

Too many believers (ten, twenty, or thirty years in their faith) still struggle with reading their Bible and praying. They haven't caught the relationship aspect of their walk with Jesus.

One-to-one disciplemaking is growing closer to Jesus, and relationships are caught, not taught. When I disciple, I share not only the foundational disciplines of my faith but also the relationship that motivates my faithfulness.

That's disciplemaking!

Never-Break Rule #4: Pray!

Jesus began His discipling ministry with prayer.

> *It was at this time that he went off to the mountain to pray, and he spent the whole night in prayer to God. And when day came, he called his disciples to him and chose twelve of them, whom he also named as apostles.* (Luke 6:12–13, NASB1995)

Developing a LampPost organizationally will always require a "connect person" to place disciplers with disciples, along with handling other organizational aspects like creating and maintaining databases, providing materials, and even organizing celebration events.

All those are important activities. But the most effective disciplemaking begins with the example of Jesus. He went up on a mountainside and prayed throughout the night before selecting the disciples who would become apostles.

We witness in the Gospels Jesus calling His disciples. There were many He could have called. Jesus interacted with thousands of people, and yet He chose twelve to be His disciples.

The winnowing of the multitude to the chosen disciples came through prayer.

I pray for people to disciple.

My prayer is simple: "Lord, show me who I should disciple next." This is a prayer that God always answers. I've noticed through years of observing the disciplemaking process that it's most successful when disciplers pray and then God connects them with a disciple.

Please note: Churches should connect disciplers to disciples organizationally. This will always be needed. But a discipler praying and God providing a disciple is most effective.

Never-Break Rule #5: Testimony!

The book of Revelation says:

> *And they overcame him because of the blood of the Lamb and because of the word of their testimony.* (Revelation 12:11, NASB1995)

Whereas preaching and worship drive attendance in a large group and interpersonal ministry keeps followers coming back to small groups, testimony best supports one-to-one disciplemaking.

In a LampPost, testimonies must be shared.

Telling stories of disciplemaking drives us from good intentions to active engagement. Our best weapon against discipleship inertia is a testimony of victory.

I've recently trained pastors in Belarus on disciplemaking through Zoom. At our last meeting, a Belarusian sister said:

> *I've found a lot of lonely people in hospitals. They lay in beds next to one another, and I asked them if I could pray for them and, often, if I could come back for discipleship. Since I'm in a ward with other patients, as I disciple, all the other patients can hear. I've led many to the Lord, and now they are discipling one another.*

There is nothing more exciting than a testimony of God working through one person to have an impact on another person for Jesus. Testimony is key for encouraging disciplemaking.

The Two Questions

Let's now answer the questions: "What do I do next?" and "What should my church do next?" Here are five specific steps to answer each question.

What do I do next?

First: Start discipling!

An ancient Greek philosopher said, "If you want to be a writer, write."

Disciplemaking is filled with good intentions. I've wondered, observing many who commit to becoming disciplers at conferences and then do nothing about their decision, if they find emotional validation by just saying that they will disciple.

And then, feeling better, they believe no further action is needed. The book of James says:

> *But prove yourselves doers of the word, and not merely hearers who delude themselves. For if anyone is a hearer of the word and not a doer, he is like a man who looks at his natural face in a mirror.* (James 1:22–23, NASB1995)

Second: Be trained and have confidence!

Foundational disciplemaking isn't complicated. That's why the phrase "I can do this!" has been used throughout this book.

All believers know about prayer, Bible study, fellowship, and disciplemaking. For older Christians, the content of foundational disciplemaking isn't new. But followers should also know a simple plan to help new believers walk with Jesus, along with knowledge and best practices for implementing this plan.

There are two pushback challenges with those considering discipleship: "I don't know how to disciple," and "I don't have enough time." With training, a discipler will learn how to disciple and learn the best practices for keeping a discipler/disciple relationship to three months.

Third: Look for an opportunity.

Disciplemaking begins with an awareness that others need to be discipled. New believers typically haven't been discipled, and neither have older followers of Jesus. Our mission from the Great Commission is to disciple those who will disciple others.

It starts with awareness.

One Sunday, in the sanctuary of the church where I was formerly the pastor, I observed someone sitting alone, so I began a conversation:

> *Me: My name is Grant Edwards. How long have you been attending?*
>
> *Sitting Alone: I've been coming here for about five weeks, though I haven't connected with anyone at the church yet.*
>
> *Me: We have what we call disciplers at this church who are willing to meet with you for ten weeks to help you know Jesus and how to have a relationship with Him. It will also help you get to know others who attend this church.*
>
> *Sitting Alone: I've seen the announcements here about discipleship. Yes, I would like to do this.*

My disciplemaking calendar was totally full, but walking past us at that time was a person whom I knew was a 3rd generation discipler. I asked this person, "Have you been praying for someone to disciple?"

The disciplemaker said, "Yes."

I introduced both the discipler and the Sitting-Alone person. Recently, I heard that the Sitting-Alone person completed *First Steps Conversations* and is now discipling another.

With disciplemaking, learning to sense a moment to make a discipling connection is essential.

When those following Jesus lack peace or experience other frustrations, it's easy to ask, "Have you been discipled?" But remember that discipleship isn't a "one and done" experience. Someone who is discipled will never get the full benefit of discipleship until that person becomes a 3rd generation discipler.

The Apostle Paul writes:

> *Conduct yourselves with wisdom toward outsiders, making the most of the opportunity. Let your speech always be with grace, as though seasoned with salt, so that you will know how you should respond to each person.* (Colossians 4:5–6, NASB1995)

Fourth: Strive for unity.

A new paradigm in a church will bring questions, cause hesitation, and challenge previous methods. Since few churches develop 3rd generation disciplers, becoming a disciplemaking church or ministry means significant change.

But there is no need for the Great Commission to cause division. Our purpose should be instruction by example, with unity as the goal.

> *With all humility and gentleness, with patience, showing tolerance for one another in love, being diligent to preserve the unity of the Spirit in the bond of peace.* (Ephesians 4:2–3, NASB1995)

Decades ago, I was sitting on my back porch, talking to the son of probably the most important cell church author of the last forty years. His son discussed how his father, after years of frustration in trying to help American churches develop small groups, moved to Asia, where a pastor embraced his ideas and then planted and grew the largest church in the world.

The son of this pioneer of cell church development looked at me and said, "Always remember that what resists a new wave in the ocean is the previous wave."

Cell groups or small groups were resisted at first by churches with large programs, Sunday schools, and Wednesday night Bible studies. Pastors and church leaders felt threatened by the decentralization caused by cell groups. They wondered what would happen to Sunday schools and mid-week Bible studies.

Integrating cell groups into the churches of America created challenges, but today, it's difficult to find a numerically growing church without small groups.

And now, the "previous wave" of small groups can resist one-to-one disciplemaking. I've heard church leaders say, "We disciple in our small groups." Yes, small groups with disciplemaking can have limited success, but one-to-one disciplemaking has better results in creating 3rd generation disciplers.

The church needs small groups and one-to-one disciplemaking—one shouldn't criticize the other.

Fifth: Become co-workers.

The Apostle Paul writes about Timothy:

> *Timothy, my co-worker, sends his greetings to you.*
> (Romans 16:21a, NIV)

What happens after three months of discipling? What type of relationship should be maintained between a discipler and disciple after going through *First Steps Conversations?*

They become co-workers. How does this happen?

After a discipler disciples a disciple, the goal for the newly discipled is to become a 3rd generation discipler—or a discipler who disciples disciplers. The original discipler can mentor and coach the disciple in finding someone to disciple and walk with them in their first discipling relationship.

The discipler and disciple become co-workers as the original disciple becomes a discipler.

> "The discipler and disciple become coworkers as the original disciple becomes a discipler."

The Greek word for "co-worker" is *synergos,* from which we get the word "synergy." Synergy joins the effort of two or more disciplers for exponential impact as they keep discipling and discipling.

The time frame should be three months to go through *First Steps Conversations* and another three months for the discipler and disciple to work together in discipling another.

This six-month guideline (two times three months) is important for three reasons:

1. It keeps a discipling relationship from becoming cumbersome and seemingly never-ending.
2. It allows the new believer to receive instruction and encouragement in foundational disciplines and an understanding of how to overcome the similar temptations that all new believers confront.
3. It enables a new disciple to quickly begin discipling. Disciples learn best when discipling others.

Now to the second question.

What should my church do next?

If a church decides to begin disciplemaking, a culture of discipleship must begin and continue.

How?

First: Preach it! Teach it! Talk about it!

Disciplemaking in a church requires constant communication. Studies indicate that if we attend a discipling conference with *First Steps Conversations,* we'll forget 75 percent of what was learned within a week.

Ouch! And the *First Steps* conference is a good one, too! What's the solution?

Please don't conclude that conferences aren't needed—that statistic also holds true for sermons! The solution is to create a disciplemaking culture by teaching, preaching, and talking about it.

A constant flow (perhaps even a barrage) of mentioning disciplemaking in a church's sermons, social media, plans, budget, and every activity is the best strategy.

When I was in high school and teaching urban kids how to swim, I learned a lesson about changing to a culture of disciplemaking before I became a discipler or knew anything about disciplemaking.

At one time, I was frustrated teaching swimming to a bunch of distracted young children. Believing that I wasn't succeeding, I asked an older instructor for advice. He asked me, "What would happen if I took this rock and threw it into the swimming pool?"

I said, "It would make a big splash." And then he asked, "After the big splash, what happens?"

I responded, "Nothing."

To which he said, "Yeah, it would settle to the bottom, and the pool would return to normal as if nothing had happened. But what happens if we keep throwing rocks?"

I quipped, "Well, if we threw enough rocks, it would fill the pool."

"Exactly," he said, "It's the same with swimming; just keep emphasizing the basics again and again, and things will change and look different."

It's probably not a good idea to practice this lesson of throwing stones next to the sanctuary's stained-glass windows, but do catch the truth of the analogy: changing a culture to disciplemaking isn't accomplished with one big splash.

Rather, it's the result of many emphasis points of teaching and example. So keep throwing rocks.

Second: Gather twelve.

If I were to hold a conference at your church on disciplemaking, whether there were twenty-five in attendance or a thousand, my prayer would be, "God, let's find twelve who will make commitments to become 3rd generation disciplers."

Not to just be discipled, but a discipler who wants to disciple others to disciple. Twelve 3rd generation disciplers will change a church!

The optimal size of a team has been studied for over 150 years. I've heard the number 4.6 often, but it's one of the vagaries of research when scholars write with a straight face that a team can have 0.6 of a team member!

I find the optimal number to begin a discipling ministry is twelve.

When praying for twelve disciplers, I have a good example with the twelve apostles. Who can fault me for following Jesus?

With twelve commitments, a church can begin a discipling ministry of six pairs discipling one another. Starting with six pairs of one-to-one disciplemaking, one or two pairs can be lost, but if all stay faithful, it's not too large a group to administer.

Before my conference at your church, not only would I pray for twelve, but I'd also ask God to bring early adopters with a passion for disciplemaking. Typically, when one-to-one discipling begins in a church, it begins with already-attending members discipling another.

After ten weeks, all twelve should ask the question, "Who should I disciple next?" The discipling ministry in a local church now has a great start. Twelve becomes twenty-four, and soon twenty-four becomes forty-eight.

As 3rd generation disciplers continue to disciple, the percentage of new believers discipled will increase.

Third: Organize.

In my community, we recently had a Chick-fil-A® move to town. Most of the evangelical pastors in our town believed it was a sign of the soon return of Jesus.

However, I didn't visit the store until six months after it arrived. My reasoning is summed up in a Yogi Berra statement that he said decades ago, "Nobody goes there. It's too crowded." I finally did visit, and I was disappointed.

Uh-oh. Please don't tell S. Truett Cathy, as I may be canceled.

How could I possibly be displeased by one of the most successful franchises in America? And I must admit that when I did visit, the lines were fast. But there was another reason it took so long for my visit.

Another former chicken franchise owner and his wife owned seven chicken franchises (not Chick-fil-A), and their food was cheaper, had a more extensive menu, and tasted better.

He (they have sold their franchises) often told me, "Through the years, we've trained thousands of young people to cook chicken. It required organization along with clear training materials."

As I've taught discipling conferences in local churches through the years, when I would ask the pastor what would happen next, I always heard various refrains of, "I'm not sure."

As admitted throughout this book, I assume responsibility because I taught disciplemaking and lacked advice on organization. That's now our focus with *First Steps Conversations*.

It's an ongoing process, but my chicken franchise owner friend also keeps telling me, "Discipleship is like cooking chicken. We want the chicken to be the same for everyone. We can organize both cooking chicken and foundational disciplemaking."

Let's cook chicken—or better yet, let's have organized 3rd generation disciplemaking in our churches.

Fourth: Celebrate!

In a recent book entitled *The Language of Disciple-Making: Saying What We Mean About Discipleship,* authors Dan Leitz and Jim Thomas write:

> *Multiplication is determined by what we celebrate and what we deem as successful. If you notice, Jesus didn't celebrate when*

20,000 people showed up to hear him teach. He didn't look around at his disciples and say, "Hey guys, do you see my crowd size?" or, "Hey team, this is what we are going for?" In fact, after they all showed up, he would often preach something hard, and people would leave.[30]

Discipleship should be celebrated specifically with individuals and churches.

For individuals:

- When a new believer completes the ten-week *First Steps Conversations*.
- When a new believer becomes a 3rd generation discipler.

For churches:

- When a group of twelve has committed to becoming disciplers.
- When 5 percent of the church's membership becomes 3rd generation disciplers.

Each church developing a disciplemaking culture will find unique and specific events to celebrate.

"Rome wasn't built in a day," and "It takes 10,000 repetitions to master a task." These statements are often shared in our culture to encourage patience and repetition. Let's add my metaphor from this chapter to these adages: "We should keep throwing stones into the swimming pool."

We become what we celebrate, and it's not one event but a continuous cycle of events that become our church's tradition. The calendar of our church should have yearly events celebrating both the vision of disciplemaking and what is being accomplished.

It's impossible to sustain disciplemaking without celebration. Don't make it complicated; keep celebrations repetitive, specific, and easy to remember.

Fifth: Emphasize adventure.

Let's admit the difficulty of change or initiating a paradigm shift in the culture of a church. It's not easy.

Consider:

A family was walking in a park when their three-year-old noticed a swing set. The little boy wanted to be swung on the swing. The father began swinging his son, but every time he tried to stop, the three-year-old started crying.

After a while, the rest of the family wanted to move on—but not the three-year-old.

Finally, the father had to drag the child off the swing. With the three-year-old still crying, the family walked around a shelter house and saw an in-ground sprinkler park. Water was shooting everywhere from nozzles in the ground.

It was a hot day, and the three-year-old quickly forgot about the swing and began running toward the water park.[31]

When we get comfortable on a swing, we can refuse to move when God wants to move on to the water park. God moves, and sometimes we stay—and then we complain about the lack of disciplemaking or spiritual maturity in churches today.

Church leaders must ask the question, "Are we stuck in the past of what God was doing?"

Scripture indicates our path with God is an adventure. Two passages about change and God's leading are valuable.

> *If we live by the Spirit, let us also keep in step with the Spirit.* (Galatians 5:25, ESV)

And Jesus said:

> *My sheep hear my voice, and I know them, and they follow me.*
> (John 10:27, ESV)

God leads, and we are to follow—keeping in step. If God seems distant, maybe He kept walking while we stayed on the swing. If God moves, He wants us to experience an even greater adventure.

I know that disciplemaking is God's adventure for the church today.

The Next Chapter of This Book

Churches haven't been discipling. Most pastors have never discipled disciplers with one-to-one disciplemaking.

Good intentions must have an actionable plan.

That's what we will discuss in the next chapter—how to develop a 90-day plan to become a 3rd generation discipler or a LampPost in a church or community!

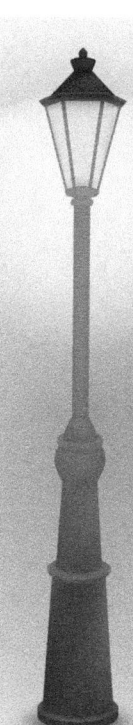

Review:
- LampPost Rule #1: Admit the problem.
- LampPost Rule #2: Know the right definition and content.
- LampPost Rule #3: Understand the blueprint.
- LampPost Rule #4: Know best practices.
- LampPost Rule #5: I can do this!
- LampPost Rule #6: Implement *The LampPost Strategy*.
- LampPost Rule #7: Foundation to Calling to Formation.
- LampPost Rule #8: Have you been discipled?
- LampPost Rule #9: God, bring me someone to disciple.
- LampPost Rule #10: A revolution starts small.
- LampPost Rule #11: The goal is 3rd generation disciplers.

Why do we have difficulty making significant changes? Discover the Wave Theory of Change in *Interlude #11*.

Interlude #11:

Wave Theory of Change

Therefore, if anyone is in Christ, he is a new creation. The old has passed away; behold, the new has come. (2 Corinthians 5:17, ESV)

It's January at your gym.

There are lots of people there—many of them new. After eating too much turkey, stuffing, mashed potatoes, and eggnog with a side of gingerbread cookies, they've lost their visions of sugar plums and need to shed fifteen pounds.

Despite great intentions, 80 percent won't make it three months into their new fitness regimes. If you're a gym regular, just be patient until March, when the crowds disappear and your gym returns to normal.

Why? Let's consider the Wave Theory of Change.

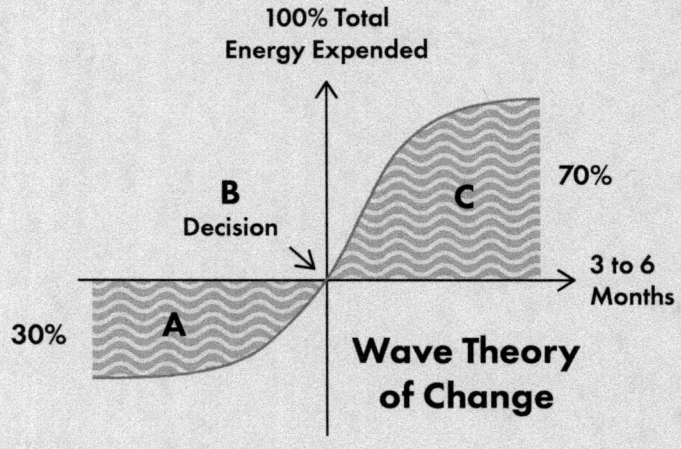

Change seldom occurs like a lazy river gently flowing with new ideas, nice and contained within the banks and not causing disruption.

No, it's more like a wave that builds in size and then explodes. But will things be ultimately different?

> A. A person knows a change must happen. It could be diet, exercise, or finding Jesus—hopefully all three.
> B. The person decides to change.
> C. After three to six months, this person is now comfortable with the change, and it becomes a sustainable routine.

Note that about 30 percent of the energy and resources required to make a change is used in deciding to change. The remaining 70 percent is consumed after the decision and change is actually made.

This explains why revivals have difficulty. An outreach organization comes to town and spends money and resources to prompt hundreds or thousands of decisions. But then the organization leaves—and invests nothing in the 70 percent required for those decisions to result in actual changed lives.

How about a person making a first-time decision to follow Jesus on a Sunday at church? This pre-follower of Jesus has spent 30 percent of their emotional energy in conviction before a spiritual change.

The decision is made, but then what?

Churches spend millions on buildings, staff, and programming to attract those desiring to make a decision. But what's the expense afterward for the 70 percent of discipleship effort needed to stabilize newfound faith?

Now, back to the gym.

Realizing that most new members will not continue to come to the gym, fitness clubs have developed a business plan that assumes this lack of attendance. One major fitness chain has an average membership of about 6,000 but with gyms that average a 300-person occupancy rate.

This isn't a good way for the church to operate.

One-to-one disciplemaking is God's business plan for the church—and God is looking for 100 percent retention.[32]

Chapter 12:

90 Days

The president of the United States gets 100 days to prove himself; you get 90. The actions you take during your first few months in a new role will largely determine whether you succeed or fail.[33]

We learn discipling by discipling. A church becomes a discipling church by discipling disciples who disciple.

My plan in ministry for helping others with their spiritual formation has always been discipleship. I discipled my wife (briefly, until I knew it was better that someone else did it); I discipled all three of my children; I discipled most of the leaders at our church; I discipled potential leaders, and I discipled leading business leaders in our community.

I believe disciplemaking helped me keep my sanity as a pastor for forty-nine years in one location.

Since I've left a full-time role as the senior pastor of a local church, I've had many conversations with pastors of other churches. I've noticed that most are experiencing various degrees of burnout and depression.

Why are so many pastors having difficulty?

Could it be the result of pastoring a programmatic church without disciplemaking? A church of many programs, staff, missions, and outreaches creates a codependent system of growth and responsibility—an ever-increasing treadmill for the pastor.

One successful pastor of a megachurch writes:

> *In America, you can be a success as a pastor and a failure as an apprentice of Jesus; you can gain a church and lose your soul.*[34]

This problem can be avoided by disciplemaking. One leader disciples another leader, and then both disciple other leaders, and the growth of leadership keeps pace with the organizational development of the church.

Leaders of ministries at the church I pastored were discipled. Knowing God's calling in their lives, they started ministries in the church from God's leading and assumed the responsibility for those ministries.

I was free to focus on disciplemaking, travel around the world for conferences, raise a family, and keep my sanity. My marriage didn't crash and burn, my children love Jesus, and the church I pastored never had a church split.

I give the credit for my success as a leader to following the simple command of Jesus to go and make disciples!

So what's the next step if you'd also like to become a 3rd generation discipler and see a LampPost of 3rd generation disciplers emerge in your church?

In this chapter, I'll walk you through the logistics of making that happen.

Start with LampPost Rule #12: Begin a 90-day cycle.

We can accomplish a lot in 90 days.

90-Day Cycles

I'm terrible with languages other than English (with English being debatable too).

When I was in the tenth grade, I was taking four classes, earning A's in Literature, Algebra, History, and Biology and an F in Spanish.

So I was surprised several years ago when I saw an ad about learning a new language in 90 days.

I was intrigued and thought, "How is this possible?" I didn't learn a new language, but I did study how the 90-day learning curve for learning a new language worked. A person can become 80 percent fluent in a language in 90 days. And yet it takes about five years to reach 90 percent fluency.

Let's consider English.

In all printed material in the English language, about 25 words make up about one-third of the material. That's right, learn 25 words, and you know one-third of a page in most books, texts, or emails written in English.

About one-half of all material written in English is composed of 100 words, and 300 words make up 65 percent. Beyond 500 words, things get more difficult because the context of words must be taken into consideration.

A similar statistic works for Russian, as 75 words make up 40 percent of what is written in Russian, and 200 words will take us up to 50 percent. In fact, this type of statistic applies to most languages of the world.

I understood how learning a language in 90 days isn't an ad-hype, getting us to purchase Rosetta Stone® (or similar) language courses. The programs focus on learning the most common words of a language and use audio instruction in pronunciation from those who speak the language.

Did you catch that important detail? *Learning a new language can be accomplished in 90 days by focusing on basic words taught by someone who speaks the language.*

So 90-day cycles can work![35]

Defining a 90-Day Cycle

I've talked with many believers who are intrigued about discipling, but despite their best intentions, they never disciple. It seems "good intentions" are an obstacle the church needs to overcome in discipling disciplers who disciple disciplers!

With discipleship, there is a "knowing and doing" gap. Do we understand the need for discipleship and intend to do something but never do?

The book of James says:

> *For if you listen to the word and don't obey, it is like glancing at your face in a mirror. You see yourself, walk away, and forget what you look like. But if you look carefully into the perfect law that sets you free, and if you do what it says and don't forget what you heard, then God will bless you for doing it.* (James 1:23–25, NLT)

We overcome this gap by making specific goals in a 90-day cycle.

In previous chapters, I explained that the three C's of disciplemaking must all be implemented at one time for 3rd generation disciplers to become workers in the harvest field.

Let's review the three C's:

1. Content
   - Foundational material
   - A discipler develops the attitude of "I can do this!"

2. Culture
   - One-to-one disciplemaking becomes a priority.
   - A discipler asks the question, "Have you been discipled?"

3. Connections
   - Disciplers must connect with disciples.
   - A discipler prays, "God, who am I to disciple next?"

A plan of disciplemaking should have a content plan, a culture plan, and a connection plan at the same time. So there is a need for the three C's of successful disciplemaking.

If there's content without culture and no ability to connect disciplers with disciples, discipleship will fail. A culture without content won't work. And if there are many wanting to be discipled with the wrong content, disciplemaking will also falter.

All three must start at the same time.

A business book entitled *Traction: Get a Grip on Your Business* by Gino Wickman has sold over one million copies. This book says:

> *The 90-day idea stems from a natural phenomenon—that human beings stumble, get off track, and lose focus roughly every 90 days. To address this aspect of human nature, you must implement a routine throughout the entire organization that creates a 90-Day World.*[36]

> *Disciplemaking should have content, culture, and connection plans at the same time.*

In this book, Gino Wickman gives two insights for a successful 90-day cycle:

1) *By limiting priorities, you can focus on what is most important. With the increased intensity of focusing on a limited number of Rocks* [his word for "tasks"], *your people will accomplish more. Remember the old saying: When everything is important, nothing is important. The way you move the company forward is one 90-day period at a time.*[37]
2) *Don't give people outside of the leadership team more than three Rocks. The responsibility is too overwhelming for most employees to handle, and you would be violating the golden rule that less is more.*[38]

We learn best in 90-day cycles. It's best to have successive 90-day cycles. And, in Wickman's terms, if we have too many rocks (tasks), the 90-day cycle can be overwhelming.

One writer who focuses on realizing potential discusses 90-day cycles and achieving goals:

> *Focused action over 90 days collapses time frames. You will achieve your goals and acquire new skills faster than you might have over a year.*[39]

When it comes to disciplemaking—think 90 days!

A Sample 90-Day Cycle for an Individual Believer Who Wants to Become a Discipler

First, find someone who wants to learn discipleship, then:

Go through the book *First Steps Conversations* with them. Develop confidence together that "We can do this!" **(Content)**

Ask God for the boldness to ask others, "Have you been discipled?" **(Culture)**

After completing the *First Steps Conversations* book, both pray, "God, bring me someone to disciple." **(Connection)**

The 90-day win: Both believers are now co-workers and begin looking for others to disciple.

Quick note: If you're a pastor and wish to see discipleship grow in your church, are you humble enough to admit you were likely never intentionally discipled? If so, you can be one of the people who go through this first 90-day cycle and launch discipleship in your church.

The First 90-Day Cycle for a Church Developing Disciplemakers

Hold a *First Steps Conversations* conference for initial training. **(Content)**

Start small and build. Pray for ten to twelve people (five to six pairs) to go through the *First Steps* conference and then commit to discipling one another. **(Culture)**

As the initial disciplers are discipling one another, organize the ministry with a Church Connector person and plan celebrations of attained goals. **(Connection)**

The 90-day win: Five to six pairs yield ten to twelve disciplers who can then start another 90-day cycle of disciplemaking, finding others who want to learn discipleship. Also, a Church Connector person is trained to organize and connect the new disciplers with disciples.

In a church, successive 90-day cycles are necessary to start and maintain disciplemaking momentum.

The Second Successive 90-day Cycle for a Church Developing Disciplemakers

Hold a LampPost conference for those who have been through the first 90-day cycle. This conference teaches the principles taught in this book and helps communities of disciplers develop other LampPosts. **(Content)**

Develop a preaching series on disciplemaking during this 90-day cycle. Also, consider graphics, social media, and other means for expanding the original ten to twelve disciplers to twenty to twenty-four disciplers and disciples. **(Culture)**

After this conference, a church now has twenty to twenty-four members learning discipleship. With the confidence of "I can do this," have them pray for someone to disciple. The new disciplers should look for a "finding a disciple" moment when they ask this question, "Have you been discipled?" **(Connection)**

The 90-day win: 3rd Generation disciplers begin to emerge. The church is not only developing multiple disciplemakers but also changing the culture from discipleship inertia to active discipling.

Finding a Disciple Moment

> *Make the most of every opportunity in these evil days.* (Ephesians 5:16, NLT)

We react appropriately to an opportunity when we've been trained to do so.

We experience a "finding a disciple" moment when we talk to someone who expresses frustration, or we sense a wobbling foundation in their relationship with Jesus. Those are moments to not just walk away, to not just say, "I'll pray for you."

Rather, they're moments to say:

I have found peace in my relationship with Jesus. I would be glad to meet with you on a weekly basis for ten weeks to go through the book First Steps Conversations. *I learned from my experience with this book to have a relationship with Jesus that gave me peace.*

We can vary the words, but when we are trained to recognize a "finding a disciple" moment we don't walk away without asking, "Have you been discipled?"

> **We don't walk away without asking, "Have you been discipled?"**

While discipling someone, emphasize that the point of the discipling relationship isn't a "one and done" experience. We want those discipled to develop a passion for disciplemaking.

The discipling experience is a joint venture of discipler and disciple becoming co-workers, and eventually, 3rd generation disciplers emerge. There is no greater feeling than God working through us to impact the lives of others.

Remember, we learn discipling by discipling. But it all starts with a "finding a disciple moment."

A Confession

This chapter gives suggestions for becoming a disciplemaker and developing discipleship in local churches.

I believe that after understanding the principles of this book and particularly this chapter, the approach taken in actual application will need to be adapted. That's okay because every church is different, and every believer is uniquely led by the Holy Spirit when discipling another person.

Your 90-day cycle can follow a plan of September through November, then rest during December and January before a second 90-day cycle spans February through April. That pattern seems to work well in many churches. Eventually, a lone "Church Connector person" might evolve into a full-time staff person, or perhaps a committee will take charge.

Do what works best—and as God directs. A motto of disciplemaking is asking God for wisdom!

> *But if any of you lacks wisdom, let him ask of God, who gives to all generously and without reproach, and it will be given to him. But he must ask in faith without any doubting, for the one who doubts is like the surf of the sea, driven and tossed by the wind. For that man ought not to expect that he will receive anything from the Lord, being a double-minded man, unstable in all his ways.* (James 1:5–8, NASB1995)

Plan each 90-day cycle by asking for wisdom. Remember that disciplemaking can become a difficult paradigm shift as your church culture changes, so pray for endurance and patience as well.

With wisdom, patience, and endurance, eventually, a local church (your church!) will have the content, culture, and connections for creative and fruitful disciplemaking.

A Mile Wide and an Inch Deep

In the 1800s, a journalist described the Platte River in Nebraska as "a mile wide and three-quarters of an inch deep."

The saying has been adjusted through the years to become "a mile wide and an inch deep" and has been used to describe something shallow and lacking depth.

I've heard this phrase in sermons and seen it in books describing the spiritual maturity of the church today. No, it is not complimentary but is probably apt—the church is shallow, lacks depth, and makes promises not fulfilled.

A mile wide and an inch deep.

The Apostle Paul prays for us:

> *And may you have the power to understand, as all God's people should, how wide, how long, how high, and how deep his love is. May you experience the love of Christ, though it is too great to understand fully. Then you will be made complete with all the fullness of life and power that comes from God.* (Ephesians 3:18–19, NLT)

Our spiritual maturity should have depth.

With an adequate foundation of content, culture, and connection, the church can disciple mature believers. Imagine churches with

90-day cycles inspiring believers to disciple and wherever they go, to ask the question:

Have you been discipled?

Twelve chapters—two more chapters to read. Before Chapter 13, let's remember what we've discussed in this chapter.

- 90-day cycles
- For lasting impact and change, a series of 90-day cycles will be needed.
- No more than three goals or tasks in each 90-day cycle.
- There should be a content task, a culture task, and a connection task.
- Starting small and increasing is best.
- Encourage disciplers in "finding a disciple" moments.

Review:
- LampPost Rule #1: Admit the problem.
- LampPost Rule #2: Know the right definition and content.
- LampPost Rule #3: Understand the blueprint.
- LampPost Rule #4: Know best practices.
- LampPost Rule #5: I can do this!
- LampPost Rule #6: Implement *The LampPost Strategy*.
- LampPost Rule #7: Foundation to Calling to Formation.
- LampPost Rule #8: Have you been discipled?
- LampPost Rule #9: God, bring me someone to disciple.
- LampPost Rule #10: A revolution starts small.
- LampPost Rule #11: The goal is 3rd generation disciplers.
- LampPost Rule #12: Begin a 90-day cycle.

Interlude #12 illustrates how we can develop a 90-day cycle for implementing disciplemaking in a church.

Interlude #12:

90-Day Cycles

Our growth can be exponential; the more we grow, the more we can grow. There is never really a conclusion; there are only new beginnings.[40]

While discussing with pastors how to begin one-to-one disciplemaking, I often hear a sigh of relief when they understand 90-day cycles.

A 90-day cycle has only three specific goals, with a win at the end.

When pastors understand what's involved in a 90-day cycle, that's when they see how quickly disciplemaking can become part of their churches.

Below is an illustration of a 90-day cycle. During the 90 days, a church needs to set only three goals.

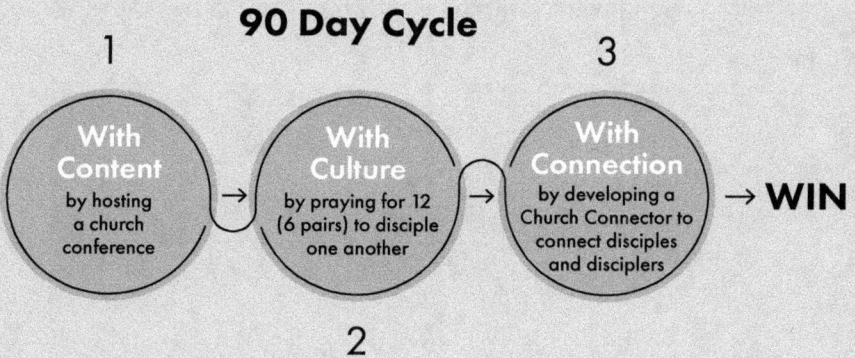

At the end of the 90 days, the win involves:

- A celebration that twelve (or a higher or lower number) have completed the content of one-to-one with *First Steps Conversations*
- Assessing what went well and what did not
- Planning for the next 90-day cycle

You read about 90-day cycles in Chapter 12, and hopefully, this illustration helps you visualize the elements of a cycle.

More than anything else, I want you to see this:

Shifting your church from one where disciples aren't made to one where they are made is simply a matter of embracing a series of 90-day cycles.

It's not a matter of setting a long list of cumbersome goals, or yet again reorganizing, or once more casting a vision that may take months or years to see take hold. It's one 90-day cycle followed by another, then another, and then another.

After each cycle, you'll find yourself breathing a sigh of relief and sensing the satisfaction of knowing you're fulfilling the command of Christ to make disciples who are launched into the world with a heart for making disciples.

So take a deep breath and say it with me: "You can do this!"

Chapter 13:

Would You Know What to Do?

Jesus intended for the disciples to produce his likeness in and through the church being gathered out of the world.[41]

I was having lunch with a local business owner recently. During our conversation, I asked him, "Have you been discipled?" He answered, "I've been a believer for over thirty years, and I've never discipled someone, nor have I been discipled."

Let's say you had that conversation with the businessman. My question for you: Would you know what to do?

And let's consider another scenario. You've just prayed with someone who decided to follow Jesus as Lord and Savior. Knowing the high probability of this person soon walking away from faithfulness:

Would you know what to do?

This book has been written so that you can answer, in both situations, "Yes, I know what to do!"

That's LampPost Rule #13: Yes, I know what to do!

Confidence

We have all experienced buyer's remorse.

It happens when we start a new adventure, a new job, a marriage, or purchase a house. Any "big" life event will cause doubt. How many of us have signed a mortgage and stayed awake for a few nights thinking, *Wow, I just committed to thirty years of payments?*

Trust me, as a person who is about to make the last payment on a thirty-year mortgage, I know about the trepidation of buyer's remorse!

Doubt and discouragement are common soon after a life decision.

But if we stay faithful, confidence builds and replaces doubt. It's too easy to have a moment of discouragement and rashly give up. We see this with new believers as they encounter a temptation or stumble and give in to the temptation, becoming so discouraged they walk away.

Same with disciplemaking!

After reading this book, you know what to do with a new or renewed believer. You can ask someone if they've been discipled, and you know how to disciple and encourage this person to not just be discipled but also to become a discipler.

Just as many had initial doubts when first deciding to follow Jesus, we could lack confidence when we sit down at our first discipling session with a new or renewed believer. And guaranteed—we will face adversity. Perhaps the disciple has a question that we can't answer or completely stops coming to the weekly sessions.

It's easy to quit or walk away from disciplemaking, but I'm asking you to persevere. The ups and downs of a discipling relationship are part of the process of becoming a 3rd generation discipler.

The book of Hebrews teaches confidence:

> *Now faith is confidence in what we hope for and assurance about what we do not see.* (Hebrews 11:1, NIV)

The original Greek word for "confidence" has shades of meaning, indicating "assurance based upon a strong foundation." We doubt when we can't see a result of our efforts in a disciplemaking relationship, and we imagine we weren't capable or didn't know enough.

Trust me, you can disciple.

First Steps Conversations is an effective tool—if you'll use it. As you do, you'll gain confidence by taking the steps to become a discipler, and then, while discipling another person, you will have some of your best, most fulfilling experiences in following Jesus.

The confidence will come, but not until you're discipling someone.

Building Confidence as a Discipler

Thinking you must succeed with every disciple brings certain defeat. I've heard disciplers quit by saying:

- My disciple didn't show up for the first meeting.
- I couldn't handle discipling an addict.
- I wouldn't give her money, and she became angry.
- My disciple and I weren't connecting that well.
- The person whom I tried to disciple became a follower of Jesus as sort of a bargain that he would get a job. When the job went to someone else, he stopped coming.

Frustrating, of course.

I approach disciplemaking with the attitude, "I don't have to succeed, but I have to try." Nobody has a 100 percent success rate as a discipler. Jesus lost a disciple, and He was the perfect discipler. Ultimately, God is responsible for success, and we only need to obey.

> *I don't have to succeed, but I have to try.*

Again, as you disciple, you'll gain confidence and become more effective. Wisdom and joy come during the process and not before.

There are ups and downs in any endeavor, and the adage "practice makes perfect" describes disciplemaking too. We learn best practices through both our victories and defeats in discipling. As we obey Jesus' command to make disciples, as we persevere, and as we learn, that's when we gain confidence.

A great example of confidence-building is Tony Romo, a former quarterback for the Dallas Cowboys football team. Let's consider:

Tony Romo's Brain

Perseverance is the key to success.

Tony Romo, a former professional quarterback, became a broadcaster with Jim Nance for CBS during the 2017 NFL season. He stood in the booth just months after having shed his Dallas Cowboys uniform.

Tony had been a good but not awesome quarterback, and his quick ascension to the CBS broadcasting booth with partner Jim Nance was perhaps the biggest victory of his professional career.

However, nobody expected much from Tony Romo, and with no former experience as a broadcaster, many wondered why he had even been hired.

During his first game, Tony did something unusual.

He would tell the TV audience—before the snap of the football—what the play would be. No broadcaster before Tony Romo had made soothsaying a part of their broadcasting repertoire. There was an obvious reason why other sportscasters kept silent: they'd look like fools if their predictions were wrong.

But predict Tony did and, often, correct Tony was.

Tony Romo impressed even his broadcasting partner Jim Nance, who, after one correct play prediction, called Romo "Romostradamus."

The Wall Street Journal featured an article about Tony toward the end of the 2019 NFL season. They wanted to check if his play-predicting ability was truly supernatural. The authors of the article watched forty-six hours of footage, reviewing every play that Romo predicted in the 2019 season.

They found that Tony had made seventy-two predictions, and he was accurate 68 percent of the time. Not quite an Old Testament prophet's percentage, but still amazing.

No, Tony Romo doesn't have a spiritual gift of play calling, but he did have two things going for him. First, he spent thousands of hours watching games and films of games, and second, he saw things in the alignment of players on the field that the fans in the stands or watching on TV wouldn't notice.

Trained as a quarterback, Tony Romo's brain worked faster than others to identify possible plays against various defenses.

And he had the confidence to pick one of those plays.

Even when he miscued a play call, his audience didn't hold it against him. He's original, likable, and humble about his mistakes. And confident enough to keep going.

Tony Romo would make a great discipler!

Yes, new followers of Jesus can disciple effectively. And as they persevere, they grow in their ability to disciple others. With experience comes the ability to sense, know, and even predict what those they're discipling are going through.

This practiced knowledge can guide your prayers, advise you, and enable you to become an amazing discipler.

My Confidence Tips

I appreciate the story about Tony Romo because I know that God has designed us to get better, to learn, and to become more effective.

When I pray for those I'm discipling, I often get a nudge I believe originates from the Holy Spirit. That and my experience spark an insight that lets me encourage those I'm discipling. Rarely does one of them face a difficult temptation without the Lord giving me a check in my spirit about what's happening. I call the disciple, and they think I'm Tony Romo.

Which I'm not; I'm just following the leading of the Spirit.

Below, I've listed my "Top Eight Tips" gleaned from discipling hundreds of disciples. They're my best practices gained from repetitive experience, honed in my personal walk with Jesus, and they have increased my effectiveness as a discipler.

By following these tips, you will gain confidence as a discipler.

Tip #1: The Ten-Minute Rule

Get started within ten minutes of sitting down for a discipling session. When we get side-tracked talking about the latest headlines, politics, or a bad call in a basketball game, the conversation begins to wander, and soon it's too late to start the session.

If discipling sessions too often include this statement, "Well, we will get around to the session next week," the discipling process loses momentum.

The ten sessions in *First Steps Conversations* contain the foundation needed for the new believer to last three months. All the sessions are needed within three months.

Tip #2: Rule of Threes

I discuss the number three often in this book.

Consider the first three months of a follower's faith. There are the three C's (Content, Culture, and Connection) for successful disciple-making and becoming a 3rd generational discipler.

I've also noticed that when I disciple someone, if we make it through three sessions, the chance to complete all ten sessions in three months increases exponentially.

I find myself praying and finding ways to encourage new believers—especially in the first three weeks of our discipleship journey.

Tip #3: Schemes of the Devil

> *Put on the full armor of God, so that you will be able to stand firm against the schemes of the devil.* (Ephesians 6:11, NASB1995)

Perhaps you've heard the phrase, "High levels, bigger devils."

The evil one is real, and your disciplemaking will be noticed by our adversary.

> *Be of sober spirit, be on the alert. Your adversary, the devil, prowls around like a roaring lion, seeking someone to devour.* (1 Peter 5:8, NASB1995)

In 1942, C. S. Lewis published his book *The Screwtape Letters*.

The book is unique in Christian literature as a fictional exchange of correspondence between the veteran demon, Uncle Screwtape, and his young nephew, Wormwood, whom Uncle Screwtape is training.

Let's read Screwtape's instructions to Wormwood about a new patient (human) assigned to him.

> *My Dear Wormwood,*
>
> *I note with grave displeasure that your patient has become a Christian. Do not indulge the hope that you will escape the usual penalties.*
>
> *In the meantime, we must make the best of the situation. There is no need to despair; hundreds of these adult converts have been reclaimed after a brief sojourn in the Enemy's camp and are now with us.*[42]

C. S. Lewis has it right.

A new believer has the attention of the demons. Fortunately, we have victory in Jesus. I pray daily for those I'm discipling, interceding for their strength during discouragement and victory in temptation.

Tip #4: It's Not Counseling!

Often, it's difficult for professional counselors to be foundational disciplers.

I hope that I haven't offended anyone.

First Steps is three months, and they're not counseling sessions. While discipling, when a new believer goes through difficulty, it's only natural for a counselor to revert to their training in cognitive behavioral therapy, asking lots of questions, breaking the ten-minute rule, and going far afield from the *First Steps Conversations* content.

Counselors and some other disciplers view whizzing past difficulties to get through a *First Steps* session as insensitive and lacking compassion.

However, the material in *First Steps* is needed during the first three months of a new believer's faith. Ignoring it to focus on problems in the disciple's life runs the risk of fixing something small and leaving the disciple unprepared for larger issues that will arise in the future. Plus, most disciplers aren't trained counselors, so it's best for them to use a script.

Foundational discipleship must be confined to the basic disciplines of the Christian faith and the similar temptations that all new believers encounter. That's what a discipler needs to do and do well. If counseling is needed, a pastor or the leader of the discipling ministry in the church (the Church Connector person) should be contacted.

Tip #5: Know How to "GAB" in Discipling

Through the years, I've developed a conversational style that increases my discipling effectiveness. I call it the GAB Method.

Let me explain the acronym.

Greet kindly, **Ask** questions, **Bless** often—or GAB.

Greet

Start every discipling session with a positive greeting.

The letters in the New Testament begin with words such as beloved, called, peace, faithful, blessed, thankful, mercy, and chosen.

It's a mistake to open a conversation with a negative or sarcastic comment or joke. That's true in life and doubly so in discipling sessions.

Paul uses the word "greet" at least twenty-one times in Romans 16. Paul was writing to those he knew well, had met briefly, or didn't know at all. The word "greet" means "to salute" or "give honor." It has more depth than a simple "Hi" or "Hello."

The first words of a discipling session set the tone of the meeting.

Ask

Ask questions often. Yes, I talk about myself, but I try to keep a ratio of 70 percent asking questions to 30 percent talking about myself.

When I ask sincere questions (sometimes several in a row), the person I'm discipling is more likely to go beyond the trivial to more serious comments. This helps our conversation be more applicable to their needs.

Bless

I rarely use the word "bless" as it seems odd to say, "Bless you, brother." That's something perhaps a formal priest might do, but it feels odd to me.

I do say at the end of a discipling session, "I'm honored that you met with me today. I will continue to pray for you daily. Let me know if you have any needs. Call anytime."

That's it; ask God to give you the ability to GAB. I believe many of you already have this gift, so just refine it a bit.

Tip #6: Memorize These Verses

If you want to elevate your discipling, memorize the key verses used in *First Steps Conversations*. They are:

- Session #1: Hebrews 11:1
- Session #2: Romans 13:14
- Session #3: Matthew 6:33
- Session #4: Romans 12:1
- Session #5: Matthew 7:7
- Session #6: Matthew 5:9
- Session #7: Romans 5:1
- Session #8: Romans 8:14
- Session #9: Romans 5:5
- Session #10: Galatians 4:28

I believe memorizing and then speaking the embedded Word of God in a discipling session has power!

Tip #7: Always Serve

The Apostle Peter writes:

> *As each one has received a special gift, employ it in serving one another as good stewards of the manifold grace of God.* (1 Peter 4:10, NASB1995)

Richard Foster, in his book *Celebration of Discipline*, writes:

> *More than any other single way, the grace of humility is worked into our lives through the Discipline of Service. Humility, as we all know, is one of those virtues that is never gained by seeking it.*[43]

Discipling provides an opportunity to serve. Never abuse a discipling relationship by asking your discipler to buy Amway® or any other network marketing product. If you sell insurance or cars or anything, do not ask the disciple to become a client.

Always be looking for unique opportunities to serve your disciple.

Tip #8: End Your Discipleship Journey with a Promise

> *Now you, brothers and sisters, like Isaac, are children of promise.* (Galatians 4:28, NIV)

How do you end ten weeks of discipling with your disciple? With a promise!

Some say there are 6,000 promises in the Bible, while others claim 1,000 promises. Let's split the difference and say there are 3,000 promises in the Bible.

They're not all for us, but many are. And those promises give hope.

There is no better way to end a discipling relationship than by having the disciple memorize 7, 13, 19. Why? Because those numbers are the passwords of living in the promises of the Bible.

With the 3,000 promises, all of them can be summarized by three ideas found in Philippians 4:

Peace

> *And the peace of God, which surpasses all comprehension, will guard your hearts and your minds in Christ Jesus.* (v. 7)

Power

> *I can do all things through Him who strengthens me.* (v. 13)

Provision

> *My God will supply all your needs according to His riches in glory in Christ Jesus.* (v. 19)

All the promises of the Bible can be summed in 7, 13, 19 or Philippians 4:7, 4:13, and 4:19. We have three promises of peace, power, and provision—disciples of Jesus are children of promise!

Remember the passwords of promise in the Bible: 7, 13, 19!

> *Remember the passwords of promise in the Bible: 7, 13, 19!*

Jesus and Peter

There isn't a better discipler than Jesus.

We won't have His perfect power and knowledge when we disciple. However, in the Great Commission, He did say His authority and presence would be with you while you disciple.

As I've developed best practices for disciplemaking, I noticed that Jesus and Peter interacted in the Gospels about seventy times. These interactions and conversations are literally a master class on disciplemaking.

Jesus, the Master, with Peter, His disciple.

I've recorded some of the discipling moments of Jesus with Peter below. Read through them while asking, "What do I learn about discipling from this interaction between Jesus and Peter?"

> *Now as Jesus was walking by the Sea of Galilee, he saw two brothers, Simon who was called Peter, and Andrew his brother, casting a net into the sea; for they were fishermen. And he said to them, "Follow me, and I will make you fishers of men."* (Matthew 4:18–19, NASB1995)

> *When he had finished speaking, he said to Simon, "Put out into the deep water and let down your nets for a catch." Simon answered and said, "Master, we worked hard all night and caught nothing, but I will do as you say and let down the nets." When they had done this, they enclosed a great quantity of fish, and their nets began to break.* (Luke 5:4–6, NASB1995)

Jesus said to Simon, "Do not fear, from now on you will be catching men." (Luke 5:10, NASB1995)

Jesus looked at him and said, "You are Simon the son of John; you shall be called Cephas" (which is translated Peter). (John 1:42, NASB1995)

[Jesus] said to them, "But who do you say that I am?" Simon Peter answered, "You are the Christ, the Son of the living God." And Jesus said to him, "Blessed are you, Simon Barjona, because flesh and blood did not reveal this to you, but my Father who is in heaven. I also say to you that you are Peter, and upon this rock I will build my church; and the gates of Hades will not overpower it." (Matthew 16:15–18, NASB1995)

Then Peter came and said to him, "Lord, how often shall my brother sin against me and I forgive him? Up to seven times?" Jesus said to him, "I do not say to you, up to seven times, but up to seventy times seven." (Matthew 18:21–22, NASB1995)

Peter said to him, "Lord, if it is you, command me to come to you on the water." And he said, "Come!" And Peter got out of the boat, and walked on the water and came toward Jesus. But seeing the wind, he became frightened, and beginning to sink, he cried out, "Lord, save me!" Immediately Jesus stretched out his hand and took hold of him, and said to him, "You of little faith, why did you doubt?" (Matthew 14:28–31, NASB1995)

Simon, Simon, behold, Satan has demanded permission to sift you like wheat; but I have prayed for you, that your faith may not fail; and you, when once you have turned again, strengthen your brothers. (Luke 22:31, NASB1995)

And Peter took him aside and began to rebuke him. But turning around and seeing his disciples, he rebuked Peter and said, "Get

> *behind me, Satan; for you are not setting your mind on God's interests, but man's."* (Mark 8:32–33, NASB1995)
>
> *Peter said to him, "Lord, why can I not follow you right now? I will lay down my life for you." Jesus answered, "Will you lay down your life for me? Truly, truly, I say to you, a rooster will not crow until you deny me three times."* (John 13:37–38, NASB1995)
>
> *And he came to the disciples and found them sleeping, and said to Peter, "So, you men could not keep watch with me for one hour? Keep watching and praying that you may not enter into temptation; the spirit is willing, but the flesh is weak."* (Matthew 26:40–41, NASB1995)
>
> *He said to him the third time, "Simon, son of John, do you love me?" Peter was grieved because he said to him the third time, "Do you love me?" And he said to him, "Lord, you know all things; you know that I love you." Jesus said to him, "Tend my sheep."* (John 21:17, NASB1995)

Jesus called Peter, changed his name, proclaimed Peter's confession as the foundation of the church, rebuked him, probably laughed with and at Peter, and forgave Peter for his betrayal.

What do we learn about disciplemaking from observing Jesus disciple Peter? We quickly note that Peter wasn't the easiest person to disciple. Sort of like me. And perhaps, like you. And definitely like some of the people Jesus will bring into your life who need discipling.

It's tempting to lose confidence if you think, "Well, it took Jesus to disciple Peter, and only Jesus could have success with my disciple."

Jesus gave us this final discipling tip:

> *Nevertheless, I tell you the truth: it is to your advantage that I go away, for if I do not go away, the Helper will not come to you. But if I go, I will send him to you.* (John 16:7, ESV)

And:

> *When the Spirit of truth comes, he will guide you into all the truth.* (John 16:13a, ESV)

Let me ask you: If the Spirit of God is with you as you disciple, does that boost your confidence? It should.

And it should allow you to say with confidence, "Yes, I know what to do!"

Chapter 14 is next, and it's our last chapter. Discipleship must have attainable goals to assess success, and it's easy to pick the wrong goals and choose the wrong metrics to measure. So we'll develop which goals are wise for you to set and consider the most important statement that we need to make to become a discipler.

Thanks for reading this book so far. Now, let's bring it all in for a landing.

Review:
- LampPost Rule #1: Admit the problem.
- LampPost Rule #2: Know the right definition and content.
- LampPost Rule #3: Understand the blueprint.
- LampPost Rule #4: Know best practices.
- LampPost Rule #5: I can do this!
- LampPost Rule #6: Implement *The LampPost Strategy*.
- LampPost Rule #7: Foundation to Calling to Formation.
- LampPost Rule #8: Have you been discipled?
- LampPost Rule #9: God, bring me someone to disciple.
- LampPost Rule #10: A revolution starts small.
- LampPost Rule #11: The goal is 3rd generation disciplers.
- LampPost Rule #12: Begin a 90-day cycle.
- LampPost Rule #13: Yes, I know what to do!

After writing this chapter that includes "confidence tips," I thought it wise in the following *Interlude #13* to explain practical steps when you sit down with a disciple the first time.

Interlude #13:

The First Meeting

Who saved us and called us to a holy calling, not because of our works but because of his own purpose and grace, which he gave us in Christ Jesus before the ages began. (2 Timothy 1:9, ESV)

Let's say that you've read this book. You know and practice the statement, the question, and the prayer:

The statement: *I can do this!*

The question: *Have you been discipled?*

The prayer: *God, bring me someone to disciple.*

You are trained, you are ready, and God has answered your prayer. You have someone to disciple. Now, you must get through the first meeting. And let's raise the tension level a bit by saying it's your first time to disciple—so it's the first meeting of the first time you've discipled.

High anxiety!

You're in good company, as I admit my own apprehension with my "first meetings," and I've discipled dozens. I've heard from other disciplers that their first meetings make them nervous too.

I remind myself before I meet someone for the first session of *First Steps Conversations* that I am walking in God's calling. Yes, there are differing callings for each believer, but all of us are asked by Jesus to become disciplers.

He has never let me down by not showing up for the first meeting. He won't stand you up, either. During your first discipling meeting, you're going to experience God working through you to impact the life of another believer!

Below is a list of three things I've found helpful as I prepare for a first meeting.

1. I begin a prayer list for my disciple before the first meeting.

It can be a simple piece of paper kept in the back of your Bible. Just list the disciple's name and the date, and start the list with this specific request:

> *"God, thank you for the opportunity to become a discipler. Give me peace and wisdom for this first session, and I ask specifically that we get through the first three sessions."*

If you get through three sessions together, the chances of making it through all ten sessions increase exponentially.

On my list, after each session, I write another date and consider a specific prayer for my disciple.

Sometimes, it's the same prayer from the week before, but I write it again. By the end of my discipling sessions, I might have four prayer requests that I continue to pray for my disciple until they are answered.

I keep praying even if the answer comes after we complete ten weeks. I find my prayer lists keep me connected to my disciples.

2. I repeat G-A-B a few times. That's right, the letters G, A, and B!

In Chapter 13 of this book, I discussed the *GAB Method of Conversation*. Again, it means:

Greet by saying something positive.

Ask questions often during each session.

Bless by mentioning a word, phrase, or attitude about your disciple that you noticed or heard during the lesson. It's good to leave the session with a blessing. Just say, "I appreciated _____ about our session today."

Learning to converse with the GAB Method greatly increases the quality of your disciplemaking. I apply the following verse in my discipling:

> *Let no corrupting talk come out of your mouths, but only such as is good for building up, as fits the occasion, that it may give grace to those who hear.* (Ephesians 4:29, ESV)

3. I look at myself in the mirror.

It would be appropriate to check for messy hair or food residue in your teeth, but I say to myself, "You can do this!" And then I add, "Jesus will be walking into this session with me!"

This might seem silly, but I believe in emphasizing the presence of Jesus in everything that I do and especially with disciplemaking. Here's one of my favorite verses for discipling. I've paraphrased it, but I think it's contextually accurate:

> *Jesus, you walk in before me and stand behind me during the entire time that I'm discipling. And during our conversations, you are placing your hand upon me.* (Psalm 139:5)

This book is about 50,000 words. I've written over 250,000 thousand other words for this book and eventually discarded and not used them. All the "kept words" included discussions about formational and foundational discipleship, how to start and keep disciplemaking in your church, and best practices.

But if you read all 50,000 words once, I pray only one thing happens in your life: you have a successful "first meeting" and many other "first meetings" too.

Chapter 14:

"Yes" or "No"?

All you need to say is simply "Yes" or "No." (Matthew 5:37a, NIV)

This entire book has been written to bridge the gap between good intentions and action.

We have the best intentions, but there is often a sizable gap between our conviction and continued action.

Believers need to obey Jesus when He says, *"Go and make disciples."* But only a small percentage will become disciplers who then disciple disciplers. While understanding the Great Commission, too many believers equivocate with excuses, postpone the starting point, or sabotage intentions with unrealistic goals.

Jesus said, *"Say simply 'yes' or 'no'!"*

The book of James agrees:

> *Above all, my brothers and sisters, do not swear—not by heaven or by earth or by anything else. All you need to say is a simple "Yes" or "No." (James 5:12, NIV)*

In this book, you have learned how to disciple and gained confidence to disciple. Now I'm asking a simple question: "Will you disciple?"

"Yes" or "No"?

I assume you just said, "Yes!" Now, let's get specific. The *Principle of Specificity* means goals within a certain time frame.

We have greater success in fulfilling our intentions when we commit to goals that are few and specific. Saying, "I'm going to memorize Psalm 25 within thirty days," works better than telling a friend, "I'm thinking about memorizing Scripture."

Specificity overcomes mere good intentions by listing timely and actionable objectives.

When I've completed a discipling relationship, I begin praying, "God, show me this week the next person that You want me to disciple." My prayer is both specific and time-sensitive.

God often answers these prayers with an unexpected encounter.

Once, on the day that I prayed about a new disciple, a man that I had never met walked into my office. After listening to his story in which he expressed frustration about his faith, I asked if he would like to go through *First Steps Conversations* and build the right foundation to experience Jesus.

I began discipling him the next week.

On another occasion, within a week of praying for another to disciple, I met a man in the line of a coffee shop. While engaging him in conversation, he told me that he was going through a divorce and that it was his fault. Weeks later, he told me that my offer for a discipling relationship, while we stood in line at the coffee shop, was proof that God still cared for him.

The Great Commission is a "yes" or "no" challenge.

That's LampPost Rule #14: Say "Yes!"

Saying "Yes" to Disciplemaking

Will you say "yes" to discipling one person a year using *First Steps Conversations*?

Chapter 14: "Yes" or "No"?

Let me define and confine my question. I'm asking that you define disciplemaking as one person a year (more if you want) and confine your discipling to the foundational content of *First Steps Conversations*.

Because you are committing to something specific, you will know if you obey. Remember, it's not ultimately important for you to succeed with every disciple—just make the attempt.

You are asked to say "yes" to a goal that can be gauged easily, with no waffling or just good intentions, but also no guilt with failed attempts. Saying "yes" is actionable. But your "yes" is essential. Agreeing to the need for discipleship accomplishes little without a specific commitment from you.

At first, disciplemaking seems like a giant leap of faith. So many questions and insecurities fill our thoughts. The following story from *First Steps Conversations* (Session #1) illustrates overcoming doubt through faith in Jesus.

> *Two friends on a weekend getaway are hiking high in the Rocky Mountains. It's a beautiful fall day, golden aspens dotting sun-washed slopes and canyons.*
>
> *Suddenly, thunderclouds roll in from the west. The temperature quickly drops as rain soaks the hikers and turns the trail slippery and treacherous. What's been the high point of their weekend has become a life-threatening nightmare.*
>
> *The hikers find themselves trapped on a ledge a hundred feet above a canyon floor, shivering, exposed to biting cold.*
>
> *As darkness falls, a chilling wind rises, and the hikers know they won't last the night. They'll die unless they get help.*
>
> *Then they hear it: a voice crying out from below. "I know you can't see it," the distant voice says, "But there's another ledge and a small cave about six feet below you. Step off the ledge you're on, and you'll land next to the cave and find shelter for the night."*

It's pitch black. The hikers can't see the cave, a ledge beneath them, or even one other.

But if they stay where they are, they'll freeze to death.

One of the hikers yells into the storm wanting to know who's there.

When the voice calls back, they discover it's a park ranger who's worked in the area for decades. It's a voice the hikers decide to trust, so they take a deep breath and, side by side, walk off the ledge.

They survive the night and are rescued the next morning.

The leap from the cliff for the two friends wasn't blind, as they heard the voice of a park ranger. This ranger knew the region where they were hiking and gave advice that could be trusted.

We are to follow the command of Jesus in our disciplemaking, and we have the promise that He will be with us. Despite our insecurities or questions of competency, we know we can trust His voice, as He wouldn't give us a command that we couldn't obey.

We can all make the commitment to becoming a 3rd generation discipler with confidence.

By the Numbers

When we disciple, how do we measure success? What metric can be used to signify that we are fulfilling the Great Commission? If we begin a discipling ministry in a local church, how do we know that we are reaching our goals?

We've heard that numbers do not signify spiritual growth. True, but where spiritual growth exists, numbers will also increase.

Correct analytics give testimony to God's power!

In my childhood church, there was a sign in the front of the sanctuary listing the last week's attendance, the offering for the previous week, and the number of baptisms for the year. Today, a church is described as a megachurch if 2,000 or more people attend. Some of the largest churches are described as "megachurches," with thousands attending in different locations.

What numbers should we celebrate? How can numbers work for us and not against us?

Metrics should gauge spiritual maturity and not just success or failure with church services. Do our statistics reflect changed lives and a church that impacts culture for righteousness—or are they a trumpet promo of our success to attract greater crowds?

I confess, as a senior pastor, I had to fight a "numbers temptation."

> **What numbers should we celebrate? How can numbers work for us and not against us?**

After examining the spreadsheets of the previous weekend's attendance and offering, if both were low, I fought frustration the entire week, and if they were high, I relished God's blessing. Numbers did that to me, bringing calm or anxiety.

That is, until I let numbers work for me by finding the one number that gave me joy.

I celebrate reading Acts 2:41, about 3,000 responding to Peter's message. I also get excited in Acts 4:4 about 5,000 more accepting the gospel, but my greatest joy is Acts 8:1, describing the persecution of the Jerusalem church when followers of Jesus *"were scattered throughout the regions of Judea and Samaria."*

When the early church was dispersed, the foundation of the Apostles' teachings enabled 8,000 believers to remain faithful and continue working in the harvest.

The large numbers listed in the book of Acts reflect the results that came from following the commands of Jesus. However, achieving those numbers wasn't an actual goal of the early church.

They understood the one number that would give them joy.

Let's Celebrate One Thing

We become what we celebrate. And because numbers are easy to tabulate, they often prompt our celebrations and, therefore, become what we consider most important.

But are ever-higher numbers the ultimate goal? The Apostle Paul didn't think so.

> *After all, what gives us hope and joy, and what will be our proud reward and crown as we stand before our Lord Jesus when he returns? It is you! Yes, you are our pride and joy.*
> (1 Thessalonians 2:19–20, NLT)

The Apostle Paul celebrates victory with the Thessalonians, saying they would be his reward and crown when he stood before the Lord. His words hint at the most important metric when it comes to discipleship. He identifies a goal that can be for everyone in your church, a unified finish line to cross, and a cause for celebration.

I believe one statistic, one goal, and one number indicate fruitful discipling. This number indicates both spiritual formation and obedience to the Great Commission.

Those are great expectations for one number.

So what is it?

First, an illustration.

A businessman recently told me:

I had been a Christian for years and even attended a Christian college. But I had never been discipled or discipled someone.

An elder of the church that I was attending asked me if I had been discipled. When I answered "no," he asked, "Would you like to be discipled?" I didn't think that I would learn anything new, but I also knew I would enjoy a new friendship, so I said "yes."

We went through First Steps, *and I realized that my foundational disciplines weren't as solid as they should be. I was challenged to recommit my faith by seeking a renewed relationship with Jesus through the disciplines of prayer, Bible, fellowship, and especially discipling.*

When I completed my discipleship, I asked my oldest son to go through First Steps *with me. At the end of our sessions together, we decided to disciple two more of my sons. He discipled one, and I discipled the other.*

Since that time, I have discipled six men, but my son, whom I first discipled, has discipled at least eleven.

I've become a 3rd generation discipler, but best of all, my son is also a 3rd generation discipler. As a father, I can't think of anything that makes me happier.

Let that sink in for a moment.

A 3rd generation discipling elder discipled a businessman, and that businessman then discipled his son. The father and son then discipled two other family members . . . and, together, an additional seventeen others.

And they're still going.

There's your one statistic, one goal, the one that indicates victory in disciplemaking and can prompt a true celebration:

It's the number of 3rd generation disciplers who are discipling disciplers in your church.

Does this mean forgetting evangelism? Far from it. A focus on discipling equips your church members to *do* evangelism and motivates them to reach out with the gospel because they feel competent to help a new convert get grounded in the faith.

Discipleship doesn't bump evangelism out of the picture—it equips believers to do it.

So let's focus on this number in the church: those who say "yes" to discipling disciples who disciple.

How many 3rd generation disciplers are in your church?

Developing a Discipling Habit

Third generation disciplers have a discipling habit.

A habit begins when a good intention becomes an action and is maintained as a lifestyle. With habits, the price of change is primarily paid during the first months of the commitment, and an established habit is maintained through the encouragement of like-minded disciplers.

While watching disciples develop into 3rd generation disciples, I've observed that the following practices encourage followers to say "yes."

Observation #1: Many hesitate at first.

At a conference with one hundred followers of Jesus being challenged to become 3rd generation disciplers, most will hesitate. That's fine because it's difficult to start with one hundred. The objective should be to start with a few and build from there.

Since developing a culture of disciplemaking in a local church is best done with consecutive 90-day cycles (Chapter 12), late adopters can always be picked up in the next cycle.

Whether you are a discipler or still hesitating, grace and peace to you—just start now!

Observation #2: Know the numbers.

Specificity fills the gap between good intentions and action. Actionable behavior is observable and can be measured. The following numbers have been explained throughout this book, and they can be used as measures of success.

- **One disciple:** One-to-one discipleship is about a discipler connecting to a disciple. This is the focal point of success in disciplemaking.
- **Three months:** Habits take at least three months, which is why most believers walk away from faithfulness in the first three months.
- **Three sessions:** Those who make it three weeks tend to go the distance of finishing the ten sessions.
- **3rd generation disciplers:** A culture changes in a church when members begin asking the question, "Have you been discipled?"
- **3.5 to 5 percent:** This is the percentage of a group that must change to start a revolution. A church should focus on this small percentage for discipling to become an unstoppable revolution.
- **Four foundational disciplines:** Bible, prayer, fellowship, and disciplemaking are the basic disciplines of the Christian faith but must have a relational context with Jesus. Our disciplines keep us on the narrow path of loving God.
- **Twelve to start:** It's best to start with small numbers when developing a disciplemaking culture. In a church, hold a conference with the goal of finding twelve and encouraging them to disciple one another.
- **80 percent of new followers** walk away from faithfulness. This statistic can be flipped to 80 percent staying faithful by developing 3rd generational disciplers. Habitual disciplers know it's God's will for them to find their next disciple.
- **90-day cycles:** Change doesn't happen in a linear manner but rather with intensifying cycles. Each 90-day cycle should conclude with a celebration and then a time of rest before another cycle begins.

Observation #3: Relentlessly encourage a "Yes!"

Often, a commitment will not be followed with action. Those who say "yes" and then do nothing can become a hindrance to others who have said "yes" and are acting on their decision to disciple.

The most vocal criticism of one-to-one disciplemaking comes from those who have never successfully discipled in a one-to-one context. A church culture of disciplemaking must strategically pursue members saying "yes" to disciplemaking without forcing the topic or becoming overbearing with those who are hesitant.

Testimonies of success are extremely helpful to maintain this balance.

Observation #4: Person of peace

> *When you enter a house, first say, "Peace to this house." If someone who promotes peace is there, your peace will rest on them; if not, it will return to you.* (Luke 10:5–6, NIV)

Whenever I've spoken about disciplemaking in a local church, whether the church is discipling or not, there is usually a person who is already interested and promoting discipleship in that church.

This is a "person of peace."

For the culture of discipling to thrive in a church, there needs to be an organizational leader. Often, God already has a "person of peace" in place who can be trained to become the "Church Connector" in the church.

Observation #5: Track the numbers—but only the numbers that matter.

Keep metrics simple when starting a discipling ministry. The three numbers to track are:

- The number engaged in a one-to-one discipling relationship.
- The number who complete the three-month *First Steps Conversations*.
- The number of 3rd generation disciplers.

Then, organize training, encouragement, media promotions, celebrations, and 90-day cycles around these analytics.

As the senior pastor of a large church, I felt my role was to enable my staff to perform their jobs. I would promote their budgets to the elders, personally deal with criticisms of their ministry, and pray for them often. My staff needed to stay focused, have confidence in what they were doing, and know that they had my support.

I followed this same approach with disciplemaking as a senior pastor. I found followers of Jesus were more likely to say "yes" to disciplemaking if they were approached with an easy-to-follow plan that was confined to a three-month timeframe.

The LampPost Strategy

Saying "yes" to discipleship is the greatest need of the church today. I pray that you understand and apply the concepts of disciplemaking in *The LampPost Strategy*.

In over five decades of asking others if they would like to be discipled by me, I've had only two people decline. Dozens have said "yes," and my disciplemaking has been the most exciting and fruitful experience of my ministry.

> Saying "yes" to discipleship is the greatest need of the church today.

Many followers of Jesus walk away from faithfulness soon after deciding to follow Him, and long-term believers are now walking away from attending church. Few churches have returned to pre-COVID-19 attendance.

A quote has been circulating recently in different media outlets from a book entitled *The Great Dechurching*:

> *More people have left the church in the last twenty-five years than all the new people who became Christians from the First Great Awakening, Second Great Awakening, and Billy Graham crusades combined. Adding to the alarm is the fact that this phenomenon has rapidly increased since the mid-1990s.*[44]

This book gives hundreds of pages of analytics describing the reasons for so many walking away from their local churches, but at the end of the book, I read this conclusion . . .

> *Belonging (or lack thereof) is the primary pain point many dechurched feel. Of all the things people said would make them likely to return, this is the greatest felt need.*[45]

The LampPost Strategy is for new believers and for renewed followers of Christ.

My wife recently completed a discipleship relationship. After the discipling sessions were complete, she asked her disciple if she would like to attend church. My wife went with her several times.

This woman whom my wife discipled recently said she keeps attending this church because she feels like she belongs—a "belonging" that began with one-to-one discipling.

Discipleship that works is about relationships.

Millions have lost a significant connection with a local church, and I don't believe a new programmatic approach will have a lot of success in bringing them back.

I do think that one-to-one disciplemaking, with both new and renewed believers, will forge those needed connections. Disciplers are needed, and I pray that you will say "yes" to discipling.

Thanks for reading this book: *Discipleship That Works: The LampPost Strategy for Disciplemaking.*

Now it's time to answer the question: Will you say "yes" or "no" to discipling?

Review:
- LampPost Rule #1: Admit the problem.
- LampPost Rule #2: Know the right definition and content.
- LampPost Rule #3: Understand the blueprint.
- LampPost Rule #4: Know best practices.
- LampPost Rule #5: I can do this!
- LampPost Rule #6: Implement *The LampPost Strategy*.
- LampPost Rule #7: Foundation to Calling to Formation.
- LampPost Rule #8: Have you been discipled?
- LampPost Rule #9: God, bring me someone to disciple.
- LampPost Rule #10: A revolution starts small.
- LampPost Rule #11: The goal is 3rd generation disciplers.
- LampPost Rule #12: Begin a 90-day cycle.
- LampPost Rule #13: Yes, I know what to do!
- LampPost Rule #14: Say "Yes!"

Endnotes

1. Comfort, Ray. *Hell's Best Kept Secret* (p. 10). Whitaker House. Kindle Edition.
2. https://redeeminggod.com/crusade-evangelism-effective/
3. Kinnaman, David; Lyons, Gabe. *unChristian: What a New Generation Really Thinks about Christianity . . . and Why It Matters* (p. 79). Baker Publishing Group. Kindle Edition.
4. State of Discipleship: A Barna Report Produced in Partnership with The Navigators, 2016 (pp. 8–9).
5. Discipleship Snapshot . . . An Honest Look From the Front Lines and Where We Go From Here. Discipleship Lab.
6. State of Discipleship: A Barna Report Produced in Partnership with The Navigators, 2016 (page 19).
7. Properly, α. **to build** (up from the foundation): Strongs NT 3618.
8. Edwards, Grant. *First Steps Conversations* (p. 83). Specificity Publications.
9. Bonhoeffer, Dietrich. *The Cost of Discipleship* (p. 203). Touchstone. Kindle Edition.
10. Watkins, Michael. *The First 90 Days, Updated and Expanded* (p. 12). Harvard Business Review Press. Kindle Edition.
11. Watkins, Michael. *The First 90 Days, Updated and Expanded* (p. 11). Harvard Business Review Press. Kindle Edition.
12. National Study on Disciple Making in USA Churches, Sponsored by Discipleship.org and Exponential. Conducted by Grey Matter Research.

13. Foster, Richard J. *Celebration of Discipline: The Path to Spiritual Growth* (p. 130). HarperCollins. Kindle Edition.

14. Guinness, Os. *The Call: Finding and Fulfilling the Central Purpose of Your Life* (p. 4). Thomas Nelson. Kindle Edition.

15. Pitman, Vance. *Unburdened* (pp. 62–63). Baker Publishing Group. Kindle Edition.

16. Melissa Fay Greene. "30 years ago, Romania deprived thousands of babies of human contact . . . here's what's become of them." *Atlantic Magazine*, July/August 2020.

17. https://www.forbes.com/sites/forbescoachescouncil/2018/11/20/why-does-culture-eat-strategy-for-breakfast/?sh=14fb8fb41e09

18. HBR Research Article . . . The Leader's Guide to Corporate Culture, January–February 2018.

19. National Study on Disciplemaking in USA Churches, Sponsored by Discipleship.org and Exponential. Conducted by Grey Matter Research.

20. www.barna.com/research/christians-more-like-Jesus-or-Pharisees

21. Kreider, Alan. *The Patient Ferment of the Early Church* (p. 12). Baker Publishing Group. Kindle Edition.

22. Willard, Dallas. *The Great Omission*. HarperCollins. Kindle Edition.

23. Willard, Dallas. *The Great Omission*. HarperCollins. Kindle Edition.

24. Willard, Dallas. *The Great Omission*. HarperCollins. Kindle Edition.

25. Kreider, Alan. *The Patient Ferment of the Early Church* (p. 8). Baker Publishing Group. Kindle Edition.

26. Gladwell, Malcolm. *The Tipping Point* (pp. 11–12). Little, Brown and Company. Kindle Edition.

27. McCullough, David. *The Wright Brothers* (p. 48). Simon & Schuster. Kindle Edition.

28. Lewis, C. S. *The Chronicles of Narnia Complete 7-Book Collection* (p. 148). HarperCollins. Kindle Edition.

29. Lewis, C. S. *The Chronicles of Narnia Complete 7-Book Collection* (p. 148). HarperCollins. Kindle Edition.

30. Leitz, Dan; Thomas, Jim. *The Language of Disciple-Making: Saying What We Mean About Discipleship.* Bonhoeffer Press. Kindle Edition.

31. Adapted from a story shared by Robert Quinn in his book, *Deep Change* (Kindle Locations 391–400).

32. I have developed this *Wave Theory of Change through twenty-five years of reading about change. I would like to thank Dr. Joseph Umidi from Regent University and Tony Stoltzfus from Leadership Metaformation Institute for their helpful insight.*

33. Watkins, Michael. *The First 90 Days, Updated and Expanded* (p. 11). Harvard Business Review Press. Kindle Edition.

34. Comer, John Mark. *The Ruthless Elimination of Hurry: How to Stay Emotionally Healthy and Spiritually Alive in the Chaos of the Modern World* (p. 4). The Crown Publishing Group. Kindle Edition.

35. http://how-to-learn-any-language.com/e/guide/vocabulary-learning/how-many-words.html

36. Wickman, Gino. *Traction: Get a Grip on Your Business* (p. 177). BenBella Books, Inc. Kindle Edition.

37. Wickman, Gino. *Traction: Get a Grip on Your Business* (p. 170). BenBella Books. Kindle Edition.

38. Wickman, Gino. *Traction: Get a Grip on Your Business* (pp. 175–176). BenBella Books. Kindle Edition.

39. Mafu, Sigu. "Five Reasons Why 90-Day Cycles Guarantee Success." https://addicted2success.com/success-advice/5-reasons-why-90-day-cycles-guarantee-success/

40. Johnson, Whitney. *Smart Growth* (p. 238). Harvard Business Review Press. Kindle Edition.

41. Coleman, Robert E. *The Master Plan of Evangelism* (p. 99). Baker Publishing Group. Kindle Edition.

42. Lewis, C. S. *The Screwtape Letters* (p. 5). HarperCollins. Kindle Edition.

43. Foster, Richard J. *Celebration of Discipline: The Path to Spiritual Growth* (p. 130). HarperCollins. Kindle Edition.

44. Davis, Jim; Graham, Michael; Burge, Ryan P. *The Great Dechurching: Who's Leaving, Why Are They Going, and What Will It Take to Bring Them Back?* (p. 5). Zondervan. Kindle Edition.

45. Davis, Jim; Graham, Michael; Burge, Ryan P. The Great *Dechurching: Who's Leaving, Why Are They Going, and What Will It Take to Bring Them Back?* (p 123). Zondervan. Kindle Edition.

About the Author

GRANT EDWARDS became a discipler within a few months of becoming a follower of Jesus.

Having accepted Jesus as his Lord and Savior on New Year's Eve 1971/1972, Grant returned to his hometown of Springfield, Ohio, where he led over one hundred hippies to the Lord within three months.

With no seminary training and dozens looking to him for guidance in developing a foundation for their faith, Grant became a student and practitioner of disciplemaking.

The ideas that he learned through study and practice led to thousands being discipled nationally and internationally.

Grant and his wife, Barbara, still reside in Springfield, Ohio, where those original discipled hippies continued to grow in number to eventually become Fellowship Church, where Grant was the senior pastor for forty-nine years.

This book, *Discipleship That Works,* is more than theory—it is lessons learned from over fifty years of disciplemaking. Learn more by visiting grantedwardsauthor.com.

Grant's core message of disciplemaking is, *"You Can Do This!"*

www.ingramcontent.com/pod-product-compliance
Lightning Source LLC
LaVergne TN
LVHW010257260326
834688LV00044B/1334